COMMUNISM

COMMUNISM

From Marx's *Manifesto* to
20th-Century Reality

Revised Edition

James D. Forman

New Viewpoints
A Division of Franklin Watts
New York | London | 1979

New Viewpoints
A Division of Franklin Watts
730 Fifth Avenue
New York, New York 10019

Library of Congress Cataloging in Publication Data

Forman, James D
  Communism: from Marx's Manifesto to 20th-century reality.

  (Studies in contemporary politics)
  Bibliography: p.
  Includes index.
  SUMMARY: Surveys the history of communism, examines the emergence and implications of Euro-communism, and considers the impact of communism on Third World politics.
    1. Communism—History—Juvenile literature.
  [1. Communism—History]   I. Title.
  HX36.F6   1979   335.43′09   78-24032
  ISBN 0-531-02933-6 lib. bdg.
  ISBN 0-531-05616-3 pbk.

Second Edition

Contents

Preface to the Second Edition   vii

Communism Defined   1

Pre-Communism   4

Early Communism   6
Karl Marx—Dialectical Materialism

Russia, the Fertile Field   10
Nicolai Lenin—The Revolution—Leon Trotsky—Joseph Stalin—
Stalinization—Nikita Khrushchev—The Present Day

The Roots of International Communism   31
The Internationals—The Spanish Civil War—World War II—
Postwar Divergence

European Communism Today   37
Western Europe—Euro-Communism—Eastern Europe—East
Germany—Poland—Czechoslovakia—Hungary—The Balkans—
Yugoslavia—Bulgaria—Albania—Romania

China, the Eastern Colossus   66
The Kuomintang—The Long March—The People's Republic—
Mao Tse-tung—The Great Leap Forward—The Cultural Revolution
—China Today

The Third World and Communism   79
    The Middle East—Egypt—Black Africa—Zaïre—Guinea—Ghana—
    Angola—Ethiopia and Somalia—Southeast Asia—Vietnam—Laos
    —Cambodia—Korea—Indonesia—India—The Future

Communism in the Americas   105
    The United States—Latin America—Mexico—Central America—
    Cuba—Chile—Political Alternatives in Latin America

Conclusion: The Emerging Future   126

Definitions   133

Biographies   137

Bibliography of Sources   141

Index   146

Preface to the Second Edition

Communism as an abstract doctrine has changed little since Marx and Lenin formulated their theories, but in the six years which have passed since this survey first appeared, the realities of world communism in its various forms have altered sufficiently to require this major revision. First there are the bastions of global communism, the Soviet Union and China. Though still suspicious of Western capitalism, the Soviet Union is now involved in the world business community, no longer confronting problems of survival but rather those of the good life, which its workers increasingly demand. China has shed its first generation of revolutionary leadership. Mao's strict dogma has begun to give way to pragmatism as more and more energy is devoted to economic rather than spiritual progress.

Throughout the Third World of less powerful nations, loyalties to one or the other of these communist giants or to the capitalistic West have variously waxed and waned. In South America, the Middle East, and India, communism has recently lost ground, while in Southeast Asia and Africa it has become ascendant. In Africa particularly, with its multiplicity of young, unstable governments, the influx of Cuban troops under Soviet direction promises uncertainties and conflict in the future.

Finally there is Europe, East and West. Among the Eastern bloc nations, which are given solidarity largely by the Soviet military presence, there is a tendency to seek individuality and establish contacts with the West. This is not a one-way street. Throughout Western Europe there is a growing acceptance of communism, no longer as a Soviet export, but home-grown and referred to as Euro-Communism. In France and Italy, where Euro-Communism is particularly strong, it has affronted international communism by setting loyalty to the nation ahead of world communism. Such are the changes which in six years have drastically altered the picture of world communism, and it is by no means a static process. Though the theoretical tenets may alter little in the next few years, dramatic shifts must be anticipated as far as their application is concerned.

Communism Defined

In 1848 Karl Marx and Friedrich Engels began their *Communist Manifesto* with prophetic confidence: "A spectre is haunting Europe, the spectre of communism." Little more than a century later, one-third of the world's population lives under governments professing communism. Yet of this multitude less than fifty million are members of the Communist party. And not one of these could realistically say that the societies that they have achieved through massive toil, dedication, courage, treachery, and blood represent true communism.

Marx took the name for his ideal society from the French communes—feudal villages that held land and produce in common. But he was not satisfied with villages. His dream was to shape newly industrialized Europe into a Communist world. As he saw it, other systems would give way or, if they fought back, be destroyed.

With the birth of the industrial age in the early nineteenth century, privately owned factories employed larger and larger work forces. The owners of these factories made vast profits, which they plowed back into building more factories. The worker was becoming a mere cipher in an anonymous crowd, alienated from the product of his toil.

Labor was hard, often dangerous, and poorly rewarded. This was the economic system of capitalism in its formative years, and Marx saw it leading only to the betterment of the owners of great businesses and to the eventual enslavement of the working class.

Marx exhorted the workers to revolt. He urged them in his writings to seize the factories from the capitalists—not to become capitalists themselves but to place the means of production in the hands of the community for the benefit of all citizens. This intermediate society controlling the means of production is called the dictatorship of the proletariat. It is what Soviet Russia and other so-called Communist nations have achieved, but it is not communism. True communism comes only with the further step of the state giving ownership back to the people, who continue to live together in abundance without supervision from a ruling class.

Pure communism does not exist in actual fact and probably never will. It is the carrot always held before the sweating mule. It is Eden come again, not only for the delight of Adam and Eve, but for every person. And much of the discussion and writing on the subject of communism has actually been devoted to the subject of the struggle to achieve socialism. Today, for the commissar who drives and the worker and peasant who pull the load, communism remains the goal still to be achieved.

Though Marx and all his disciples have insisted and continue to insist that socialism is only a way station on the road to communism, they have not dared to describe this final paradise on earth except in the sketchiest terms. With the final achievement of communism, greed and competition are supposed to cease. All people will contribute according to their ability and receive according to their need. There will be no cause for crime or vice of any kind, no race or class rivalry, no grounds for war, and no reason for government. However, this ideal state of communism is no nearer to being realized today than when Marx first conceived it. Today's Communist leadership would no sooner tamper with the writings of Marx and Lenin than the Church fathers would update the Old and New Testament. Yet as science hampers a literal interpretation of the Bible, so too have communist realities strayed from the sacred word, no more alarmingly perhaps than in regard to Euro-Communism.

Marx saw communism as a class struggle transcending national boundaries. Lenin and Stalin accepted this theory, adjusting it so that Moscow would remain the capital for the movement world-wide. Ethnic and national bonds have for the most part proven stronger than party loyalty, but never with more outspoken intent as expressed in behalf of the new doctrine of Euro-Communism. Throughout Western Europe Communist leaders are professing democratic loyalty to their particular national state, an affront to traditional party orthodoxy as serious as Martin Luther's theological heresy in the 16th century.

If the trend is honest and flourishes, Euro-Communism may be the beginning of a rapprochement to democratic socialism which has prospered for years in several European countries. These other socialist nations do not necessarily regard their present systems as the end to socioeconomic evolution, nor do they postulate communism as a necessary next or final stage. Britain, where capitalism began, now operates largely under a socialist system. Slow evolution by way of free election has been responsible for this continuing change. Communists reject such democratic socialism, maintaining that a system with more than one political party inevitably permits the confrontation between capitalists and workers. They feel that a small party of convinced Communists must steer a socialist society in the best interest of all the people.

For the purposes of this study to discover the situation of communism in the world today, we will consider three basic elements as characteristic of a Communist state. First, there is state ownership of the principal means of production. Second, there is totalitarianism, with government control firmly in the hands of a minority—in this case, dedicated Communists. Finally, there exists the messianic purpose: the eventual establishment of the ideal world community called communism.

Pre-Communism

Since Adam and Eve were cast out of Eden, people have dreamed of a return to earthly bliss. When this hope was abandoned, religion offered a paradise after death, a qualified and often dubious substitute. In ancient Greece, Plato hypothesized in his *Republic* a perfect state, which was to be ruled by philosophers and protected by a class of dedicated guardians. Wealth and education were to be communal. But Plato did not have the industrial age to deal with, nor did he eliminate from his ideal state class distinctions or the institution of slavery.

Ancient Rome both in its republican period and later under the emperors always supported a strict class hierarchy. But one strongly communistic effort came from a slave, Spartacus, who led a rebellion of slaves against the Roman legions and very nearly prevailed. During the brief years of this insurrection, the embattled society of slaves existed in a communist type of community. And Spartacus remains a hero in Soviet literature.

England contributed its pre-Marxists. In the sixteenth century, Sir Thomas More wrote of an imaginary island country where all property and produce were socialized. He called it Utopia, from the Greek word for "nowhere," and Marx in his time found fault with it because More offered no scientific steps for its realization. John Locke, the classical economist, saw all people as possessing property in their own person: that is, the labor of their body. But Locke was thinking of farmers and artisans and not of the factory worker to come. Substituting action for words were the Levellers, a group formed of rebel soldiers during the English Civil War. Their goal was to take away the estates of the rich for the benefit of peasants and artisans. But the Levellers were before their time, and their movement never received wide support.

A most influential social thinker of the eighteenth century was the Frenchman Jean Jacques Rousseau, who published *The Social Contract* in 1762. This work advanced the idea that people could attain harmony by making a social contract among themselves, remaining their own sovereigns after the contract was made. Rousseau's thoughts were acted upon by the instigators of the American Revolution and were even more responsible for the French Revolution that followed. Its goal was not socialist. But the French Revolution remains a landmark in the march of socialism, for it destroyed a monarchy and became an impetus and a warning for future revolutionaries.

Early Communism

From popular rebellions and the Napoleonic Wars that followed, Western Europe, led by Britain, stumbled into the Industrial Revolution. It was a new game without rules. And if one were wealthy enough and ruthless enough, one became a capitalist. Unscrupulous capitalists hired factory labor to work the new machinery, paid the lowest wage possible, and had no responsibility for injuries on the job. There were no such things as social security, sickness pay, or labor unions. The workers lived in ignorance and squalor and had no prospects beyond long hours of toil and an early death. It wasn't long before the voice of reform was raised by such writers as Charles Dickens. It was with the attitude of a charitable and repentant Scrooge that Britain moved toward labor reforms and socialism.

Karl Marx   The process of reform was slow, and its voice was not loud enough for Karl Marx. He was born in Trier in the Rhineland, Germany, the son of a lawyer of Jewish descent. Marx studied at the universities of Bonn and Berlin, becoming first a devoted follower of the German idealist Georg Wilhelm Hegel and then a radical social philosopher obsessed with a desire to improve the lot of the worker. In 1847, working in Brussels with the help of Friedrich Engels, Marx wrote the *Communist Manifesto*. It was published the next year. These were years of turmoil in Western Europe. And Marx found himself expelled from one country after another until settling in London, England, which became his intellectual haven for the rest of his life.

The *Manifesto,* a brief pamphlet, contained a summary of Marx's whole social philosophy and sounded to an unheeding world the first trumpet of world revolution to come. Nineteen years later the first volume of a weightier three-volume set would appear, entitled *Das Kapital.* Together with the *Manifesto* and lesser writings by Marx and Engels, it became the communist scripture, the most influential writing of the nineteenth century. The goal these works announced was the emancipation of the laboring man from the economic tyranny of the capitalist few. In building their theoretical explanation of the way in which history and economics function—a theory they called dialectical materialism—Marx and Engels relied on the following major principles.

Dialectical Materialism   The first principle in the scheme is historical determinism, meaning that history is governed by natural laws, which the mind can ascertain and which make it possible for man to interpret the future. Second come the laws of history themselves. In this part of his thinking, Marx was much influenced by Hegel, who had seen the historical process as one of opposing forces whose struggle leads to change. Hegel called this process of historical change the dialectic. Marx urged revolution when social structures reached a stage at which change was inevitable.

Coupled with this third notion of violent historical struggle is the fourth point: Marx's economic interpretation of history. Marx saw that beneath all historical change, ideas, institutions, laws, even religious practices, the evolving economy was fundamental. This concept was related to classical materialism, which defined people and nature as fixed products of natural law. But Marx went further in his final principle of dialectical materialism by proposing the idea that through the economic struggle it is possible for people to master the world they live in and to improve it. The whole process of history for Marx was a continuing struggle between hostile economic interests. The conflict, as he saw it developing inevitably in the nineteenth century, matched the increasingly wealthy capitalist class against the increasingly numerous and deprived workers. The Marxist system offered both a means of understanding society and a program for changing it.

All this Marx conceived as certain to occur. As capitalism perfected itself technically, the supply of available goods produced would gradually outrun customer demand. The result, Marx predicted, would be a decline in profits. And the grasping capitalist would make up his losses at the expense of the worker who was obliged to sell himself, not for the value of what he could produce, but for the value of his labor as established by the capitalist. Clearly the latter's profits were in conflict with the former's wages, and sooner or later a class struggle had to result.

Marx could not imagine bourgeois capitalists voluntarily giving up their privileges. So he advocated violent revolution. The first practical step would be the formation of political parties and trade unions of workers. Once organized, the workers would revolt. By sheer force of numbers, they would take over and impose their will under a dictatorship of workers, otherwise known as the proletariat. With the important means of production as well as the government in their hands, a state of socialism would exist. During this time, publicly owned industry would gradually absorb smaller producers. Such ownership in common would eliminate the profit motive, and the economy could be planned for the future good of society. With competition and selfish motives eliminated, everyone would benefit materially. And as everyone's material environment improved, so human nature would improve. The state, as policeman, would gradually lose its function, and the dictatorship of the proletariat would fade away into a classless society. In this millennium, the final and perfect historical stage in Marx's scheme, all economic and hence all related struggle would end. People at last would be free to employ their faculties to the limit.

Marx imagined a perfect future, but the obstacles were many. Parliaments, kings, and a tsar ruled in Europe, all anxious to maintain their power. In the East there was very little industry and, therefore, no army of workers to revolt. During

COMMUNISM

Marx's life, Britain, Germany, and France were the capitalistic strongholds. It is in these countries that Marx envisioned his mission being achieved. But even at his own level of struggle, there were opposition and disunity. There were socialists, less radical than himself, who wanted peaceful change. These Marx dismissed with contempt. There were anarchists who, like himself, dreamed of a stateless society, but one very different from his. The anarchists simply planned to burn down the government where it stood. But because they lacked an organized plan, he dismissed them, too.

Marx was a philosopher, not an activist. Apart from his writing, he undertook only one important organizational activity— the leadership of the International Workingmen's Association, beginning in London in 1864. This group has since been referred to as the First International. It lasted twelve years and was a failure. The Second International was called together in 1889, after his death, and it lasted until World War I. Its blunt attack was concentrated on the industrial West, and it ignored tsarist Russia almost entirely. After all, Russia had few industrial workers, only rural peasants, and a tiny core of intellectuals stifling under tsarist tyranny.

Russia, the Fertile Field

Tsarist Russia was a vast, backward country overrun for centuries by the Tartars. It lay forgotten during the Renaissance and the Reformation that illuminated Western Europe. Capitalism began flexing its muscles in England when feudalism prevailed in Russia. But change began peacefully enough with a flowering of the Russian intellect. Tolstoi and Dostoevski were among the writers who complained of injustice to the masses. On March 3, 1861, Tsar Alexander II, autocrat of all Russia, abolished serfdom. It was the right and honorable thing to do, but it came at the wrong time. The right time had long since passed. This mere taste of freedom, without the economic changes necessary to make it meaningful, created more discontent. And although the tsar remained personally respected by the peasants, he became the target of attempted assassinations by the radical, alienated youth. On March 13, 1881, a nihilist radical wounded one of the tsar's Cossack guards with a bomb. Alexander mildly reproached the would-be killer as the police held him, and then he thanked God aloud for his escape. "It's too soon to thank God," shouted a second fanatic as he hurled a fatal bomb at the tsar's feet.

Nicolai Lenin Alexander III, who had watched his father die, opposed all revolutionary movements and built up his police force. A man named Alexander Ulyanov was hanged for an alleged plot against the tsar. His brother, Vladimir, a young man of twenty-one at the time, swore blood revenge. In time he would change his name to Nicolai Lenin. He would have his revenge, not against Alexander III, who died peacefully, but against his weak and vacillating son, Nicholas II. As early as 1904, things were going very badly for Nicholas. He was losing a war to Japan, and unrest was simmering in Moscow. In the next year, a protest march occurred that resulted in bloodshed and would be remembered as Bloody Sunday. All over Russia, the workers' councils, called soviets, which were to be so useful to Lenin in later years, began massive strikes. Government officials resigned, and anarchy reigned. Nicholas was driven to concessions. He agreed to a parliamentary government—of the most limited type—and the following year the first national elections in Russian history took place. Russia seemed on the verge of entering peacefully into the twentieth century.

It was not to be. The tensions that make for historic change, by no means all of them Marxian, were building up in Western Europe. Marx's *Das Kapital,* forecasting capitalism's fall, had long since entered Russia, passed by censors who considered it incomprehensible gibberish. However, a young idealist, Georgi Plekhanov, found it inspiring reading. In 1883, he left Russia for Switzerland, where he formed a group of Russian Marxian Socialists.

Meanwhile, Nicolai Lenin was preaching against the government. His efforts were rewarded with exile in Siberia. A few months after his term of exile had expired, he too went to Switzerland and joined the Russian Social Democratic Party. At first he deeply respected Plekhanov. But disagreement came after a short time. Remembering his brother's death, Lenin insisted on revolution led by a vanguard of revolutionaries. This was Lenin's first practical contribution to the Communist cause. He did not think it was likely that the Russian working class as a whole would ever spontaneously develop class consciousness. He devised the idea of a hard-core elite, dedicated revolutionaries who would supervise and indoctrinate the workers while infiltrating decadent capitalist institutions such as the army and government bureaus.

This theory of the professional revolutionary bound to his

fellows by military discipline appeared in Lenin's first really influential pamphlet, *What Is To Be Done?* It was published just after the turn of the century. The idea of the professional revolutionary constituted a real departure from Marx, who had devoted his efforts to developing mass trade unionism. By 1903 Lenin's doctrines had split the party into two factions. The Bolsheviks, literally meaning "the majority," followed Lenin. The minority, or Mensheviks, retained the traditional Marxian view. Among the Mensheviks was one Lev Bronstein, who preferred the name Leon Trotsky.

The Revolution　Heedless of the petty wranglings of minor eccentrics, Europe prepared for war. This came as a relief to Tsar Nicholas, for patriotism increased in Russia, and even the socialists supported him. The Russian Army, however, was far from ready, and against the Germans it achieved one spectacular disaster after another. While the army sank into defeat and demoralization, the peasants at home were starving. Bread riots took place. In 1917 tsarist soldiers fired on the protestors, and then the army began deserting to the people. The revolution had begun spontaneously and without leadership. Returning from the battlefront, Nicholas found his path blocked by revolutionaries, and in a railway car at Pskov he was forced to abdicate on the spot. A moderate government led by Prince George Lvov and Alexander Kerenski was formed, while far away in Switzerland Lenin hopped about in forgotten frustration. Only when the moderates in power in Russia decided to continue the fight against Germany did Lenin's chance come. He persuaded the Germans that he would work to get Russia out of the war, and for that purpose they sent him home in a sealed railway car with the slogan "Peace, Bread, and Freedom." On April 16, 1917, he arrived in Petrograd.

A moderate, bourgeois government was the last thing Lenin wanted. He took his Bolshevik doctrine to the workers with another slogan: "All power to the soviets." He didn't mean it, but the undisciplined workers and soldiers were susceptible to the persuasion of demagogic slogans. And Lenin managed to disrupt more conservative efforts at forming a government.

However, when an election was finally held to form a lasting government, the Bolsheviks did badly. Lenin took courage from Aristotle's doctrine, "Revolutions are effected in two ways, by force and by fraud." He found questionable grounds to ignore the result of the vote. Since his elite was better situated and better organized than the opposition, he took control as though the vote had been an endorsement. The following year, 1918, the Bolshevik party was reborn as the Russian Communist party.

There was still substantial opposition, from both right and left. The royal family had to be shot. The divided army fought among themselves. But the Communists occupied central Russia and had the support of the peasants. While Marx had foreseen the emergence of his ideal society in Western Europe, where the proletariat would rise in an already industrialized state, Lenin was absorbed by the great expanse of Russia, a land dominated by peasant farmers. His determination to harness them to the Communist revolution was his second important addition to Marxian theory. By way of incentive, he promised to give them the land of their former lords.

Even with the mass of peasant support, the civil war sputtered until 1921. Then the capitalist world, which had given sporadic aid to Lenin's conservative opposition, wearied of the war. Russia herself was exhausted, but the progress of Communist consolidation could move ahead. It was a staggering task in a poor land, made poorer by more than six years of killing. But it was undertaken by bold, capable, and ruthless men.

In theory, the Marxian formula was to be followed. But where Marx had imagined a proletariat spontaneously conscious of its historic mission, he had never clarified what he meant by the dictatorship of that proletariat. Lenin had never had illusions about the ability of an unorganized mass of workers and peasants to generate a successful revolution. He had even less expectation that they could consolidate the results. So into the formula "dictatorship of the working class" he introduced a substitution. "In behalf of" replaced the preposition "of." He might speak of democracy, but the immediate implication was far from traditional. The word meant to Lenin, at most, the mass participation of the Russian people. It did not imply free elections or the existence of more than one political party. It meant totalitarian socialism with himself at the top as dictator, administering the country through a central committee comprised of dedicated Communists down through a widening pyramid of party functionaries to the final cellular units.

In fairness to Lenin, he did not conceive of this governmental structure as perpetual. Rather, he regarded himself and his elite followers as a team of surgeons operating on a sick patient, Mother Russia. With the operation a success, the patient would presumably recover. The surgeons would withdraw, and Soviet Russia would experience the truly democratic life of the stateless Communist millennium.

Although problems within war-ravaged Russia were monumental, Lenin did not overlook the fact that the Communist revolution was a worldwide undertaking. Here, again, he modified Marx, who had concerned himself only with industrialized capitalist countries. Ironically, the backbone of the Russian Revolution had been the peasants. In other European countries, where factory workers were proportionately stronger, Communist revolutions had failed dismally. The implications would have been shattering for a strict doctrinarian, but Lenin was a pragmatic realist. If peasants rather than industrial workers rallied to the Communist banners, that was fine. With this in mind, it was Lenin who first enlarged the Communist world movement to include underdeveloped nonindustrialized countries where no true capitalism and no class struggle, in the Marxian sense, existed.

Leon Trotsky   Lenin was not to live long enough to see how well this change in emphasis served world communism. Barely had the major industries of Russia been nationalized when, in March of 1923, he suffered a paralyzing stroke. Within the year, Lenin was dead. His obvious heir was Leon Trotsky. Trotsky was a university graduate, a dynamic and heroic product of the revolution, a man who had known the privation of banishment to Siberia. He had followed the Mensheviks during the early party split, rejoined Lenin in 1917, and created the Red Army while Lenin took over the government.

Joseph Stalin   Like so many early Communists, Trotsky's strongest rival for power, Iosif Vissarionovich Dzhugashvili, went under an assumed name. Its English translation had a comic-strip tone—"Man of Steel." In Russian, it was "Stalin." Despite the name, this amiable, plodding party worker who always voted with the majority seemed no threat. Yet Trotsky and Lenin had never much liked the man. And before his death, Lenin had been planning to have Stalin fired from his post of general secretary of the party on the grounds of "rudeness." This was revealed in Lenin's testament dedicated to his wife, Krupskaya. But Stalin suppressed the document and consolidated his power.

The son of a shoemaker, Stalin had been expelled from a seminary for radicalism in 1899. He'd joined the underground under the name Koba (meaning "the indomitable") and had gravitated to the Bolsheviks in 1904. Later he became the editor of their official newspaper, *Pravda.* In the revolution he was unimportant and no match for Trotsky intellectually. But where Trotsky was a theorist, Stalin was a dogged opportunist and organizer. Stalin was willing to take routine jobs that bored his colleagues. None of them seemed to realize he was building a fortress within the party through gradual control of the secretariat and various commissions, by systematically removing from office friends of Trotsky and replacing them with his own followers. Later Trotsky would comment in his book *Stalin:* "He is needed by all of them—by the tired radicals, by the bureaucrats, by the kulaks, the upstarts, the sneaks, by all the worms that are crawling out of the upturned soil of the manured revolution."

Apart from the sheer quest for power, the two men differed fundamentally on the future course of the revolution. Trotsky, the optimist, saw the revolution progressing democratically with the cooperation of the workers. Stalin, a bureaucrat by nature, lacked confidence in the regime's popularity. With the help of his allies in the politburo, the controlling executive committee of the Communist party, Stalin kept Trotsky from a commanding position.

Another issue between them concerned international communism. Traditionally the world movement came first. But Stalin insisted that Russia could build a Marxist society in Russia without the support of the proletariats of other countries. Trotsky clung to the traditional international emphasis. But his view became less popular as international communism in the 1920s met with no success. Must the Russian Revolution be dragged down by the failure of communism in other lands? Stalin denied it, and his was the brighter hope.

Trotsky was at first considered to be in error. Then he was viewed as a heretic. And one by one his offices were stripped away. In 1927 he was driven from the party. Hounded into exile, he moved from country to country, ending up in Mexico. He was finally fatally attacked there on August 20, 1940, by Stalin's agents, and died the next day. All who espoused Trotskyism courted a similar fate.

While Marx had theorized the revolution and Lenin had brought it about, Stalin was left to harvest its fruits. He had the party and the machinery of government behind him. The Communist party, regarded as the vanguard of the working people in their struggle to strengthen and develop the socialist system, had a monopoly of political power in Russia. Without a rival, it still describes itself as democratic on the premise that the elimination of class rivalry in Russia had eliminated any need for diverse representation. Therefore the party—made up of about a million members out of a population of 194 million in Stalin's day and over 12 million from a population of 250 million today—holds power over public policy and foreign affairs.

Ruling the party itself is the politburo. It, in turn, is subject to the will of the general secretary, who was Stalin as long as he lived. The party, of course, required governmental machinery. This consists at the upper levels of a congress of soviets, called the Supreme Soviet, which administers legislative power through two chambers. From its members is elected a presidium under a chairman. Like the party, the power structure is pyramidal, and it was subject in the final analysis to Stalin's will.

Stalinization   For Marx and Lenin, the world revolution had come first. For Stalin, it was simply a tool to serve the interests of Russia, which he intended to build into an industrial fortress and a strong nationalistic state. Where Lenin's "dictatorship in behalf of the proletariat" had been strict, Stalin's rapidly became absolute. To make Russian communism succeed in a watchful world of capitalistic enemies, the first need was industrial power. With major industries already in governmental hands, Stalin had no need to depend on the growth of a free market. He owned the means of production, and he simply told the factory heads what and how much he expected them to produce. To this end, economic goals were set for a span of five years. This was the first of the so-called five-year plans. Stalin ruled over its administration like Ivan the Terrible.

Lenin had already destroyed the power of private business people and landowners in order to create a manageable industrial army; but even Communist workers had to eat, and they weren't eating much. The peasant farmers, with nothing in the way of consumer goods to buy, were sensibly eating their own produce instead of selling it. During the early days of communism, famine had gripped the land. Half a million people had died. Lenin had been forced to establish a new economic policy allowing farmers to keep the land they had appropriated from their landlords and sell the produce from it.

By 1928, agriculture was gaining ground but doing so noncollectively, and Stalin needed more food for his factory hands. It was unthinkable to trade with capitalist countries for consumer goods that would have induced the farmers to sell their produce. And Stalin's government lacked the funds and the patience to negotiate with the peasants. The alternative, from which Stalin never flinched, was ruthless force. In the process, he even concocted a scapegoat for Russia's failure to move more rapidly toward paradise on earth. He insisted that all the fault lay with the more wealthy farmers, the *kulaks,* whom he labeled capitalists in disguise. In practice, a kulak was any farmer who resisted Stalin's new policy of agricultural collectivization: that is, the seizure of privately owned farms by the state, for the purpose of lumping them into larger state-run farms upon which the former owners worked as strictly supervised employees.

Collectivization reached its peak in 1939. Stalin had proved he could take away the land, but he could not make the survivors work. It was not until the mid-1950s that Soviet agriculture recovered. Meanwhile half a million farmers died by violence or starvation. Millions were deported to Siberia. Somebody had to work the mines there, and few would do it from choice. With industrialization still in the future, it was expedient to have a good supply of "state criminals." There were strange Communist heroes in those days. Typical among them was young Pavlik Morozov. Evidently young Pavlik had an unresolved Oedipus complex, for he denounced his father for saving out a little grain from the collective. The father received ten years in Siberia, and his son a statue in Moscow's Krasnopresnensk children's park.

Organizing the farmers not only accorded with proper theory, it also had the short-term objective of getting food to the factory workers. Industry moved ahead at a fantastic rate in preparation for the inevitable war against capitalism and the millennium to follow. It mattered little in the larger scene that hundreds of thousands in the Ukraine and Northern Caucasus starved to death, along with one-third of the livestock in all the country. That was the price, and Stalin was prepared to pay it.

Many old comrades of the revolution, some who had loved Trotsky, others who were pure Marxists, objected to this process of Stalinization. Some may even have plotted against Stalin. It was enough that he thought so, and in 1936 he began the great party purge. Confessions, true or falsified, were extracted by force. One implicated many. Like some medieval witch-hunt, victims were found in one government department after another. The end finally came amidst the police themselves. Appropriately, the last victim claimed was the chief of police, Yezhov, after whom the purge, the *Yezhovshchina,* had been named in the first place. Literally thousands of top officials were executed in the last years before World War II. Stalin emerged supreme, without challengers, but in doing so he had violated another basic Communist rule. He had set the individual above the party, tying its fortunes to the life expectancy of one man rather than to the enduring corporate entity of communism itself. Not until after Stalin's death did anyone dare to point out this fact.

While the Yezhovshchina had strengthened Stalin within the party, it very nearly finished him and the rest of Russia in the bargain, for the army had been purged of its best commanders and totally demoralized. When Hitler attacked in 1941, Stalin's defeats dwarfed those endured by the tsar twenty-seven years before. But the savagery of the German invaders turned many potential defectors into staunch patriots, and the vastness of Russia gave the country time to rally. It had workers and citizens with a deep love of their country. And the Communists made full use of nationalist feelings. Russia's new industry, together with foreign aid, particularly from the United States, gave her the weapons to resist. Her victories in the end were complete, and Stalin survived the war, respected not only at home but around the world, as the good, benign "Uncle Joe."

The glow was quick to fade as discord arose between Russia and the Western powers over the partition of Germany, particularly regarding its capital city, Berlin. Communist subversion began to infect the nations of Eastern Europe. The United States countered with massive military aid to the countries in the West. In Korea, American soldiers fought against their former allies, the Chinese Communists. And the warm global cooperation of World War II became the cold war of suspicion. Old Communist world dreams were reasserted, and Stalin breathed the air of vast power. Things had changed since the early days when he had been a hunted bank robber and political fugitive. Military expenditures mounted, atomic bombs were tested, and the world seemed once again on the brink of war. Then, suddenly, on March 5, 1953, the "Man of Steel" died.

Nikita Khrushchev   No one man could replace Stalin. Malenkov, Molotov, and Levrenti Beria, chief of the secret police, ruled together. The trio broke up in July, 1953, when Beria was removed from his offices, and on December 23 was executed. His police were demoted as a power, and in time the size of the labor camps was cut back. Less violent jockeying for power continued until Nikita Khrushchev stood alone. An old party hand, peasant by birth and in manner, Khrushchev brought with him an earthy charm and a return to the atmosphere of pre-Stalin days. In an address that shook world communism to its roots on February 24, 1956, Khrushchev denounced Stalin for his "cult of the personality." He cited his crimes, such as the execution as counterrevolutionaries of 1,108 of the fewer than 2,000 delegates who had attended the seventeenth party congress. Communism would return to the methods of Lenin, he said, which involved persuasion and explanation.

Changes were quick to follow. Authority, at least among the 12 million party members—in a population of 200 million people—was decentralized. Concessions were made to the peasants, and Stalin's plan to place agriculture totally in the hands of state-run communes was revised. More consumer products appeared on the market. Even for dissident intellectuals there was more freedom, though critical novels—such as Dudintsev's *Not by Bread Alone*—were attacked. And Pasternak's *Doctor Zhivago,* which was to become famous and win for its author the Nobel prize for literature, had to be printed and distributed abroad. The steps toward liberalization were small, but at least they moved away from the complete totalitarianism of Stalin's day.

Internationally, change under Khrushchev was more dramatic. While Stalin had awaited inevitable war and the dying outburst of decadent capitalism, Khrushchev spoke of peaceful coexistence and control of the arms race. These overtures did not mean that he disavowed eventual Communist conquest —not at all. In fact, he widened the cold war. While Stalin had generally limited his range of domination to those lands that his armies could physically control, Khrushchev saw communism's victory being won through economic aid, persuasive example, and indoctrination. Africa, Asia, Cuba, South America, the whole underdeveloped world needed help and guidance. And, following Lenin's insight, Khrushchev was determined it should come from a Communist source.

Then on October 14, 1964, Khrushchev was out—neither tried, nor shot, nor imprisoned, but abruptly and completely retired, left to die in peace. The reasons were various: mismanagement of the Cuban missile confrontation, an economic crisis at home, and his own efforts to secure total political power. His violent denouncement of Stalin was also an important factor, for it had disrupted Communist parties all over the world for whom Stalin had long been a god. It also discredited Russian communism in general and Stalin's still-surviving associates.

This move against Khrushchev did not indicate a complete revival of Stalinism, but it led to the covering up of an unsavory and embarrassing past, which has recently been further glossed over by the appearance of a modest, fatherly statue of Stalin in Red Square. When some dissidents gathered there to protest any ceremony honoring the ninetieth anniversary of his birth, no ceremony took place, nor had one been intended. Disappointed, the protestors got into an argument, and a banner bearing Stalin's portrait fell to the ground. A poet, Anatoly Yakobson, who was near the fallen flag, was arrested, charged with behaving foolishly on Red Square, and fined ten rubles. One of Yakobson's friends commented, "We are delighted to hear of this law, for our group has always opposed foolishness on Red Square." Clearly, though, Stalin has reappeared, raising the question: Is he only a harmless ghost or is he reincarnated in the form of Leonid Brezhnev?

The Present Day   In 1977 Soviet Communism celebrated its sixtieth anniversary. It had reasons to be proud: a growing economy, world power, with warships sailing the seven seas, over forty other countries looking to the USSR for financial aid. But there is a price on success. No longer is there room for that revolutionary mentality of everything to gain and nothing to lose. Khrushchev's flamboyant gambling over Cuba would no longer be tolerated, and the general tone of his successor, Leonid Brezhnev, has been that of prudent expansion. He is a bureaucrat born of Russian socialism, so dull it is difficult to remember what he looks like, industrious, discreet, businesslike, but no fiery revolutionary.

Internationally, caution has set the tone of recent years. In 1965, when the United States was deeply involved in the Vietnam war, there was talk of enlisting Soviet volunteers for the North Vietnamese army. They did not materialize. And where direct confrontation has since threatened, appeasement has been resorted to with the goal of maintaining international stability. The key word is "détente," meaning a relaxation of strained relationships. Strategic Arms Limitation Talks (SALT) have continued doggedly in the hope of restricting nuclear arsenals.

There are two schools of thought that purport to explain this growing conservatism. The older theory attributes it to the United States and its allies and their efforts to contain the USSR. Without such vigilance, communism would quickly surge ahead toward world domination, and this view is not without a measure of truth. Even putting the old dogma of world revolution aside, a country which saw some 20 million of its citizens slaughtered in World War II must be excused for a certain pathological fear of invasion and overcompensation in terms of military power. The more recent theory, and one that is gaining validity, holds that along with de-Stalinization, Soviet world ambitions have modified. In Russia, there is growing skepticism. If our collective farms don't work, they ask, and our centralized industries have problems, should we recommend our system abroad? In keeping with this attitude was the popular joke of the early 1960s after the poor wheat harvests, when wheat was purchased from Canada: "Why do we have the most brilliant farm experts in the world? Because they plant grain in Kazakhstan and it comes up in Saskatchewan." Under Stalin, making such a joke would have been suicidal. In 1975 the joke was even more valid, when a disastrous grain harvest was eased by vast purchases from the United States. Stalin would have preferred to see his peasants starve rather than accept such humiliation. Brezhnev felt obliged to swallow his hard line pride and accept the deal as good business. If nothing else, the Soviet Union has come to recognize Western capitalism as the pacesetter in world commerce. Russia needs and wants up-to-date computer technology and a share in the world trade market. By 1970 Russia was operating 28 foreign-based business enterprises. Seven years later they had grown to 84, and each such investment, as it depends on world peace, is a counterweight to the old dogma of revolution.

Although erratic weather can take much of the blame for periodic Soviet crop failures, communism has never been a real success in the agricultural sector. Efforts to apply Marxist ideology to natural science has in the past had as bad an effect upon food production as upon those scientists who argued that growing things do not respond to political theory. The classic example of this party line pseudo-science involved Stalin's pet biologist, Trofim Lysenko, who repudiated genetics and insisted that characteristics acquired from the environment could be transmitted in the evolutionary process. For twenty-five years Lysenko ruled supreme while any vocal dissenters languished in prison. Chronically, half the combine-harvesters are out of order by spring, and come autumn, soldiers and even Moscow students have to be recruited to harvest potatoes and beets, making collective farms sound more like disaster relief than efficient modern agriculture. Yet ideologically the collective farm is so fundamental to communist doctrine that they persist against the evidence that privately owned farm plots, while accounting for but 1 percent of agricultural land, yield 27 percent of the total value of farm production. Somehow industrially oriented Communists have been slow to grasp the fact that all East European peasants have an even older and more tenacious desire to work their own land. Despite the anathema of private enterprise to communist theory a gleam of light showed through when the October 1977 constitution stated: "The law permits individual labor in handicrafts, farming, the provision of services for the public and other forms of activity." This new attitude was confirmed recently by an article in the Communist party newspaper *Pravda* lamenting an urban trend which adversely affected the private ownership of pigs while state farms have been condemned for purchasing private livestock to make up for their own inadequate production. So it is with near glacial slowness that farmland moves back into private hands or is worked under looser state control.

Industry, too, is undergoing change. In Stalin's day, there was a surplus of unskilled labor. Now such labor is short. People are more valuable, and the demands of a more complex economy force doctrine to give way to flexibility. Khrushchev did a great deal to break down the strict, centralized control of factory management that had existed before. To organize a workers' group in opposition to management or to contemplate a strike, activities central to formative communism, would still land a man in prison. But at least the individual has a chance of changing his job or of registering complaints through prescribed channels. These were dangerous, often impossible liberties during Stalin's day. Unfortunately this liberalizing trend has been too rapid for the conservative Brezhnev, who called for a tightening of state controls, more ideological exhortation, and stricter work discipline. As yet, they have had very little success, and the Soviet economy is in trouble. Five-year plans set in 1976 for economic expansion already, in 1978, show every sign of falling far short of their objectives. Heavy industrial output has the lowest goal for any year since World War II. Steel production, regarded as a barometer of Russian progress, is scarcely expected to expand at all. Living conditions remain poor. There are shortages of consumer goods that the public demands. Even if the leaders wanted to, they could not return to the Stalinist past, nor can they deny certain economic facts of life as Marx and Stalin tried to do.

For Marx, only labor created values. Therefore, any factory profit above wages was capitalist exploitation, so invidious a term that any such profit appearing in Soviet factories was labeled "surplus value." The measure of a factory's success was not whether it achieved a profit margin in a market depending upon supply and demand but whether it lived up to the "demand economy" set by the government. For each factory there was a quota: for example, ten million bricks or one million tons of locomotives. If the quota was not achieved,

COMMUNISM

spies and foreign agents were blamed, and the managers were fired. To avert this, the brick factory might achieve its quota by suddenly changing over to smaller bricks, the locomotives plant to making ponderous, rail-crushing engines. And it took a bold manager indeed to ever halt production in order to install new, and in the long run, more productive technology.

Despite communist dogma, the logic of economics exerts strong pressure toward decentralized control, a market sensitive to consumer choice, and success measured by surplus value (or profit) instead of simple output. Khrushchev was aware of these facts of economic life, but his successor, conservative doctrinarian at heart, has tried to put on the brakes to stop or at least slow the rate of change.

With the spread of education so necessary to an advanced industrial society, a tentative intelligentsia has appeared in Russia. Though in no position to seriously threaten the Soviet monolith, these few daring thinkers have at least questioned communist ideas that formerly were never questioned. While the present party bosses would hesitate to use guns against their striking workers, they have been heavy-handed in dealing with dissent, ever since the brief flowering of freer literature under Khrushchev. Consequently, a vast underground literature called *Samizdat*—"self-publishing"—has been hand-typed and circulated. It has led to unrest and a tightening of control. In 1968 several writers, among them Aleksandr Ginzburg and Yuri Galanskov, received prison terms of five and seven years for "upsetting" the Soviet community. In 1974 Alexander Solzhenitsyn, winner of the Nobel prize for literature, was expelled from the Soviet Union for his opinions. The visual artist has a bit more leeway than the writer. Portraits, still lifes, and landscapes inherently are nonpolitical. Should the artist paint a robust lumberjack felling a tree, the Ministry of Culture would guarantee sales and throw in an additional annual stipend. On the other hand, if the artist's wood gatherer were a threadbare peasant woman piling twigs into a baby carriage, the state might well take offense and ban the work. Few Soviet artists have sought out such confrontations. Though admitting a political limitation on the subject of his art (most modern art is considered "decadent" and therefore forbidden public exhibition), one patriotic artist pointed out rather fatuously that he was not on the other hand commercially enslaved by the necessity of making a living, as is the case with the Western artist.

Though in 1975 the Helsinki accords were signed, calling for the free movement of peoples and ideas, Russia has done nothing to implement the terms, and dissent has fallen to a low ebb. In connection with the sixtieth anniversary of the Soviet Union in 1977, an amnesty for prisoners pointedly failed to include prisoners of a political nature. One may observe, however, that this is an improvement over the past. Stalin would have had the lot of them shot. But it is still far from the tradition of individual freedom and liberty accepted in the West. A most chilling method of dealing with such intellectual deviants has been to pack them off to a mental home, wrap them up in wet canvas, inject them with drugs, and house them with the genuinely insane until such time as they return to their party-line senses. Such frightening tactics are reminiscent of Hitler, Stalin, Tsar Nicholas I, and many of the latter's predecessors.

For anyone accustomed to Western freedoms, the situation in Russia would be intolerable. Opportunities for choosing one's own employment are limited, and to work purely as an individual is almost impossible. Foreign travel is limited to the highest party members. Religion is officially regarded as an impediment to the attainment of true freedom of conscience— yet it remains a powerful force among large elements of the population. So in practice a priest who limits himself strictly to church matters, mass, confession, baptism, is not interfered with. But when religion enters into everyday life, as with the fundamentalist Pentecostal sect, its members are harassed and humiliated. Yet with all this, the Russian citizen of today can look back on a blacker past and say: We are not starving. No one will come to shoot us in the night. In general, the courts of the Soviet Union deal out fair and folksy justice. A man can be heard, even if now and then the laws are changed to raise the penalty after the crime has been committed, a sort of ex-post-facto treatment that would turn an American judge's hair white.

An example of the difference in attitude between the Western democracies and the Soviet Union, between the emphasis on the individual and his fulfillment as opposed to the fulfillment of the state, often at the individual's expense, occurs in the Russian's so-called Parasite Law. Under this law, anyone who is not gainfully and usefully employed for the good of society may be uprooted from his home and sent to a specified location where work will be provided. Candidates for this administrative extralegal punishment include pimps and prostitutes and anyone who gets drunk regularly or works irregularly. There are merits in such a proceeding. How quickly the streets of New York City could be cleaned up by regimented vagrants! But there are grave dangers. What does a court define as useful employment? Does it include critical writers? Avant-garde painters? Or does it not?

Nevertheless, the Soviet Union has come a long way from the serfdom of just over a hundred years ago. A counterrevolution today is unthinkable. True, there is some discontent, but not so much because of the limitation of freedoms known in the West that few Russians have ever experienced. Rather, it is an unhappiness at the continued low standard of living, poor and limited housing, the unavailability of the material plenty that is known to exist elsewhere and that might be more available to Soviet citizens if the command economy were directed away from enhancing a powerful state to providing its individual members with the comforts of life. There is little disloyalty. The people don't want to overthrow their government. They simply want more out of it. And at the top there is a very complacent aristocracy, not one established by birth and automatic inheritance, but by party devotion and ability.

Russians today still like to voice the old formulas of Marx and Lenin. They have reason for pride in the emergence of a great nation and cause, too, for disillusionment with their ideology, which has become but a thin crust spread over a very large pie. In theory, they are a classless society, yet a ruling clique has emerged within the institutional embodiment of the party. And what may be spoken of as the dictatorship of the proletariat is, in fact, the dictatorship of a new Soviet bureaucracy. Such government in the hands of official administrators, who are free of the popular will, is as un-Marxian as the profit motive in industry. The fact remains that from the point of view of income alone, a vast gap is developing between the government officials, executives, and scientists on the one hand and the workers and peasants on the other. For those with money and influence there are stores, accessible only to holders of special passes, featuring otherwise unobtainable luxury goods. This is an example of discrimination that would have every civil rights group in the United States out howling in the streets. And there are many among the less privileged in Russia who no longer swallow the propaganda of total equality and who look upon the well-dressed party members with growing, if still silent, bitterness. With a maximum income tax of 13 percent as against 70 percent in the United States, the actual difference between rich and poor is wider and still widening. Once again, Marx has cause to turn in his grave.

Though energy supplies are becoming a concern, as they have been for some time through the rest of the industrialized world, the Soviet Union has relatively boundless economic potential. Russia is a vast, underdeveloped country, with enormous natural resources. The only real question is whether its leaders will adhere to inflexible and inhibiting doctrine in its development, or whether there will be a slow drift toward a market economy and perhaps toward democratic socialism. As wealth increases, so will individual expectations and demands upon the part of the intelligentsia as well as the general public. Such demands are not likely, however, to threaten the structure of the Soviet state, for Russians have been accustomed to a tightly run bureaucracy since the days of the tsars. The intelligentsia will easily absorb the ablest children of the masses without revolution or purge. Unquestionably there will be a diminution in ideological fervor, but in a nation accustomed to untold generations of tyranny in one form or another, even under the most optimum conditions it will be a long time before the average Russian will learn how to cope with genuine democracy.

Industrialization in Russia has already begun to bend slightly toward Western methods. The process may be very slow, and it will be resisted on the part of entrenched and conservative government. But there are courageous spokesmen such as the hydrogen bomb physicist Andrei Sakharov, who dared publish an open letter criticizing the quantitative and qualitative lag in the Russian economy. He speaks of the second Industrial Revolution and calls it a Western phenomenon, with particular reference to the computerized methods of the United States. In his view, industry must be decentralized. Information must be exchanged internationally, or Russia will stultify in its plodding, unimaginative bureaucracy. Lesser heroes than Sakharov might well be put under psychiatric care for such statements, but the Communist party's only revenge was to deny him permission to travel to Oslo, Norway, to receive his Nobel prize in 1975. Who will prevail? The bureaucrats, mouthing old formulas and guarding a closed society, or the muffled intelligentsia, confident that Soviet Russia can flourish as a more open society?

Whatever happens, a return to Stalinism is as unlikely as is the traditional communist goal of a classless society. A popular Soviet anecdote says: "Communism is just over the horizon, but the horizon is an imaginary line and as you approach it, it recedes." The truth is the Soviet Union is becoming a country, not a cause, and at the November 7, 1977, sixtieth-anniversary parade honoring the birth of the Soviet Union, Defense Minister Marshal Dmitri Ustinov was undoubtedly speaking for the vast majority of Russians when he justified the display of military might by saying, "So that no one will dare disturb our tranquil life." The revolution is over in Russia. Visionary power has died and political ideals are largely relegated to the classroom. Brezhnev has given the country 14 years of stability with old style totalitarianism gradually giving way to a more tolerant authoritarianism. But Brezhnev and his colleagues are aging. His health has been questioned. Presently a new leadership must take over. In general, they are better educated, less ideological. This next generation of leaders may be experimenters in reform and liberalization, though initially they may, to solidify their positions, have to take a tough, even militant stance. Nevertheless, peace is fundamentally desired, as is world trade and Western technology, and with it all must come a spilling over of the Western life style. The Soviet Union has long been a model for communism around the world. It may remain so. But though its power is unquestioned, its desirability as a model for emerging nations depends on its ability to keep up with the times.

COMMUNISM

The Roots of
International Communism

Before the Russian Revolution, communism had been a world-oriented movement. Marx himself had presided over the First International Workingmen's Association, with delegates coming to the meeting from many European countries. Another such international congress sputtered along from 1889 until World War I, urging on the struggle for world communism. Its achievements were minimal. Russia, of course, was communism's first real success. But war-ravaged Europe of the early 1920s saw other "socialist" uprisings. In Hungary, Communist insurrection had to be put down by the invasion of armies from other nations. In Munich a bloody revolt was easily crushed. In those days, if a Communist were asked, "For whom are you most willing to die, world revolution or Mother Russia?" the correct answer was "world revolution." Not for long, however; at least, not on the part of a Russian Communist. In 1919, while the Revolution still sputtered, the Third International was called. No longer a convention of workingmen, it was in truth the first Communist international convention. It adopted the name Comintern. And under this name Soviet Russia would manipulate Communist infiltration and subversion throughout the world for the next twenty-four years.

The Internationals Although the membership of the Comintern was worldwide, clearly Soviet Russia called the tune. One year later, at a second world congress, it set out twenty-one strict conditions that Communist parties throughout the world had to accept or be banished from the movement. Typical were the following: to fight reformism; to form nuclei in trade unions and capture them from within; to seek peasant support; to promote emancipation of colonial peoples; to purge petty-bourgeois elements. Of vital importance was weeding out the non-Bolshevik left, the "opportunists," as Lenin called them, who did not look to Moscow for direction.

During the 1920s, Communist parties throughout the world responded to the Soviet Union, accepting from the various international congresses more and more organization along Russian party lines and fighting their isolated and generally unrewarded battles against the governments of their respective countries. All the while, fascism—the political system in which all power lies in the hands of a dictator whose purpose is the achievement of national or racial supremacy—was growing in Italy and Germany. In the latter country, the Communists were so myopically involved in undermining the Social Democratic party that they were completely unaware of Hitler and his Nazis until it was too late.

Alienation from the world community reached its peak during the years 1928–1933, when Stalin had cemented power at home and called for a hostile, disruptive effort abroad. Then, in a reversal, while at home Soviet Russia purged its kulaks and commissars, a brief sunshine fell on the international movement, with a new unity of purpose in opposing the growing threat of fascism. The idealistic days of the Popular Front were launched with the Seventh International Congress, which met in the summer of 1935. At the Congress, Russia announced the radical about-face to the other national parties. No longer were they to work against their governments. Instead, they were to popularize world communism as a patriotic, open, cooperative organization bent on resisting tyranny and oppression. The shift from subversion to cooperation left most of the delegates bedazzled at first. But, like the responsive puppets they were, they carried the news home. The about-face was achieved immediately, and in most cases with profound relief at the prospect of knitting together a divided loyalty.

The Spanish Civil War The great test between communism and fascism was not long withheld. In the summer of 1936, a series of politically motivated murders in Madrid gave the final excuse to the fascistically inclined Spanish Army, with the general support of the aristocracy and the Catholic church, to revolt "in the interest of the Spanish people" against the shaky Republican government. An army coup in Spanish Morocco was led by General Franco. Quickly the rebellion spread to Spain. Most workers and peasants rallied behind the official government. Battle lines formed, and the first real revolution in Europe since 1919 was launched with all the Spanish ferocity that had once frightened Julius Caesar.

Fascist Italy and Germany plunged in with men, arms, and airplanes, on behalf of Franco. The Western democracies officially aided neither side. Russia, however, came to the aid of Republican Spain, where communism had been a weak and splintered party. Stalin had more than one reason for involvement. First, it was a chance to move the center of anticipated war far from his own vulnerable frontier. More obviously, it was an opportunity for the spread of international communism. While stingy with arms, which he sent along only at a stiff price, Stalin generously sent out political advisers and military instructors, for it wasn't victory alone that he wanted, but a Communist victory. When Republican successes suggested victory through negotiation, Stalin saw to it that his Communist officers initiated a disastrous and pointless offensive. Through such tactics, Soviet communism gradually changed what had been a Fascist versus Republican war into a confrontation between fascism and an alliance of liberals, Republicans, and Communists that was dominated by the Communists.

Japan was meanwhile mounting a threat to Russia's Asian back door. Purges in the Russian party had reached a bloody peak, and aid to foreign shores was no longer practicable. Republican Spain, now politically divided by Communist manipulation, was left to die and with it thousands of idealistic young "Communist" volunteers from a number of Western democracies. Even the United States was represented by "the

Abraham Lincoln" and another brigade. This was the naive period, when to many, international communism seemed to be the hope of the world. It was a period that would not come again.

In late August 1939, the ideological skies darkened abruptly when Soviet Russia, the champion of antifascism for the past five years, announced a mutual defense pact with Nazi Germany. Suddenly the new enemies of communism were Polish landlordism and British and French imperialism. The violent reversal was too much for even some hard-core Communists to take. For some of the survivors of the Abraham Lincoln Brigade and their spiritual cousins, it was the cynical end of the rainbow. Membership in world communism dwindled until the early summer of 1941, when, suddenly, Germany attacked Mother Russia. Out went the shock waves. In her peril, Moscow announced the great patriotic war of democratic nations against the Nazi tyranny.

World War II International communism fell into line once more, but the innocent dedication of the Spanish days had gone. For those to whom communism had been an ideal dream, there would always remain the disturbing memory of the Soviet-Fascist pact, but the balance of the war served communism well. Disillusionment within Russia became submerged in patriotism. So tremendous was her effort at self-preservation that the Soviet Union emerged from war a mighty world power. Communist-dominated resistance movements in Eastern Europe, China, and Indochina also prospered. Communist resistance fighters in Eastern Europe emerged as patriots and heroes.

War cast a rosy glow on the Grand Alliance. In 1943, the Comintern was dissolved in form, if not in fact. And the illusion began to emerge in the West of democratic nations living in harmony under the supervision of a paternal United Nations. Such a hope was of short duration. With victory, the glow was quick to fade. Tensions developed. And in 1947 the Cominform replaced the Comintern as the guiding body for international communism. Superficially it concerned only the Communist-dominated countries of Eastern Europe and the promising Communist parties in France and Italy. But in fact its influence was very little changed from that of the Comintern. However, the Cominform achieved no more success than its predecessor, and in its turn it, too, dissolved. With the demise of Stalin, the intensity of rocket-rattling regarding the disposition of Berlin and the Korean War began to diminish, and it reached a new low with the Cuban missile debacle of 1962.

Khrushchev initiated a period of winning friends via massive aid programs to underdeveloped nations. This, too, has diminished. Apart from arming various Arab countries, this indiscriminate aid program has largely been replaced by more subtle and less costly diplomacy, in an effort to achieve small advantages without calling forth major reactions. One example of this new diplomatic approach has been the effort at rapprochement with West Germany.

The Russian drive toward world revolution, the old idealistic dream, has lost much of its luster. Soviet Russia now seeks primarily to consolidate itself as a world power. Allies are no longer restricted to by-the-book Communists, and to this end the Soviets have achieved much success but met with problems. Among the latter are a lagging economy, a restive Eastern Europe, and unstable Arab friends. The Kremlin, like the White House, is haunted by doubts, not the least of which relates to her most powerful and all-too-eager heir, communist China.

Postwar Divergence In Marxist theory, international discord is caused by capitalist imperialism. Among Communist countries, "fraternal peace" is expected. It seemed to exist between China and Russia back in 1949, when Chairman Mao visited Moscow in the hope of solidifying relations while at the same time persuading the Russians to return machinery confiscated from Manchuria during the war. Moscow was agreeable all around, and Mao went home speaking of the "internal and indestructible" friendship between the two countries. Traditionally, however, no matter how repugnant to Communist theory, there has always been enmity between the two. In Russian eyes, China has always represented the yellow peril as typified in the popular joke about the Soviet and Chinese diplomats who were discussing the latter's population problem. The Chinese diplomat suggests that perhaps it might be solved by moving a few Chinese to sparsely settled Siberia. "What do you mean by a few?" asks the Russian. "Oh, perhaps 80 or 90 million for a start," comes the reply.

Since 1949, the traditional fear and enmity between Russia and China has found doctrinal channels. Of particular importance has been the divergence of world views. Russia came early to speak of competition rather than conflict with the capitalist countries, while Mao coined the slogan "Political power grows out of the barrel of a gun." Until a few years before his death, Mao insisted on a Communist hegemony achieved by violent means. Then, through personal diplomacy involving a rapid thaw in Chinese relations with the United States, the principal capitalist bogeyman, even Mao modified his militancy, as have his successors.

A one-sided world, all democratic capitalism in the Western sense or all communism, achieved by either violence, subversion, or overwhelming competition, seems increasingly less likely. Islam and the Catholic church, though once bitter enemies, have both sturdily survived centuries of crusading, and so undoubtedly will the opposed and evolving ideologies of the twentieth century. This is not to deny that communism has already made rapid progress, not so much toward the Marxist millennium as in terms of territorial control. It will be the purpose of the forthcoming chapters to evaluate the communism in that territorial spread, both in its theoretical and in its practical aspects.

European Communism Today

Western Europe Historically and philosophically, communism developed out of Western European culture. There Marx confidently expected capitalism to run its violent course in the leading industrial nations. No such revolution has as yet taken place. And though in France and Italy leftist coalitions have shown growing strength at the polls, a genuine revolution in support of a world Communist movement is now less likely than when Marx was writing.

In practice, Marx's theory that the advance of industrialization would lead to increased exploitation of the worker simply operated in reverse. As industry prospered, so did the worker. In England, where capitalism was born and where Marx wrote his anticapitalist books, the Communist party remains legal, but it has done its reputation more harm than good by a miserable showing at the polls. Superficially this can be explained by the fact that the mass of British workers faithfully support the Labour party, which is vigilantly anticommunist. The real reason is democratic socialism.

Unlike communism, this political theory was never based on violence, had neither a rigid plan nor a dogma, but rather relied on the motto "Reform without resentment." In its early days, the movement was led by a group of sober intellectuals, such as George Bernard Shaw, Sydney and Beatrice Webb, and H. G. Wells, who called themselves the Fabian Society. Devoted to democratic socialism, Britain's Labour party enjoyed a steady growth at the polls until it became a majority party. Many of its goals have been achieved, such as the nationalization of several major industries and services including coal mining, electrical power, gas, and national health. The return of a Conservative government is not apt to occasion many backward steps. The success of democratic socialism and the failure of communism in Britain suggest that freedom is a better weapon against communism than repression.

Vigorous Communist parties still exist on the Western European continent. But for the most part they are well-fed Communists. Their interests are better served by labor union action within the community than by risking all on overthrowing society. Furthermore, they have learned through bitter experience that international communism as directed from Russia serves Russian objectives, with complete indifference to local considerations. Toward the goal of reconciling the Communist party with national self interest, something new has emerged in the mid-1970s, and that is "Euro-Communism."

Euro-Communism "Workers of the World Unite" was Marx's and Lenin's monolithic slogan of the past. This common purpose of forcibly remaking a brave new world free of capitalism was still being voiced in the 1960s. But at the 1976 International meeting in East Berlin, Communist delegates from Japan, Britain, Spain, France and Italy proclaimed themselves attached to democratic principles and parliamentary institutions, while accepting alliance with noncommunist political parties and rejecting dictatorship of the proletariat and proletarian internationalism. All this runs counter to Leninist dogma.

In Spain, Communist party leader Santiago Carrillo put the word in print with his book, *Euro-Communism and the State,* in which he accused the Soviet Union of stifling human rights and holding back economic progress. Then in the autumn of 1977 the Italian Communist party went so far as to set up communications with other West European socialist groups in the hopes of establishing a cohesive group of like-minded parties. These proposals included such died-in-the-wool democratic socialists as the Scandinavians and the always Soviet-wary Finns. While British Communists total only some 25,000, two of their members, Mike McGahey of the Scottish miners and Ken Gill of the engineering workers, have risen to union leadership by renouncing world revolution in favor of a broad democratic alliance of labor.

In two countries, France and Italy, this new Euro-Communism is of particular relevance, for in both the Communist party is strong and close to sharing governmental power. Georges Marchais heads France's Communist party. He began as a slavish follower of the Moscow line. Then, in 1968, he denounced the Soviet invasion of Czechoslovakia, and in 1971 condemned the treatment of Jews in Russia. The following year he was repudiating revolution as a way of reforming France. By 1976 it seemed a very likely probability that in coalition with the larger Socialist party, led by François Mitterrand, the Communists under a "common program" might by 1978 be elected to power for the first time. Now that the brief honeymoon seems to be over, the primary issue is the nationalization of French industry. Inconveniently for both Communists and Socialists, French capitalism is a real success under the center-right government of President Valery Giscard d'Estaing. The more moderate Socialists have in mind nationalizing only 9 firms while the more radical Communists would take over some 1,400—a discrepancy of such magnitude as to be irreconcilable. On March 19, 1978, came the trial of strength, and the French voter who likes to talk radically but vote conservatively retained the old center-right government coalition by a majority that stunned the leftists and at least temporarily halted the advance of Euro-Communism in France.

In Italy the Christian Democratic party has been the core of every Italian government since the end of World War II. But Italy today does not share France's economic success. Unemployment is dangerously increasing, and inflation is rampant. The police are intimidated by youthful Communist terrorists, the Red Brigades in the north and the Proletarian Armed Guards in the south. The management of public institutions and big private enterprises have been disrupted by their excesses, to which not even the official Communist party gives support.

In the constant turmoil, Prime Minister Giulio Andreotti's Christian Democratic party has lost confidence and dwindled to about 38 percent of the voting public. Meanwhile, the Communists, organized into an effective mass organization by Palmiro Togliatti and now led by Enrico Berlinguer, have increased their support to 34 percent of the voters by playing down their traditional atheism in a Catholic country and denying any design to nationalize industry. In July of 1977 the Christian Democrats, together with the Communists and lesser parties, signed a "limited legislative agreement" on broad principles for maintaining public order and achieving economic social reform. Yet the situation continued to deteriorate. In January 1978, the prime minister resigned under pressure from the Communists as well as from the Socialists and Republicans. Recalled, Andreotti has formed Italy's thirty-ninth postwar regime. Though he contrived to deny the Communists the cabinet seats they desired, he was obliged to promise reforms and include them officially as part of the majority. While in the past they abstained, now they must be asked to vote for government measures. The result is that Italy has moved a step closer to the first major experiment in Euro-Communism.

Although undoubtedly the most significant recent development in the evolution of Communism, Euro-Communism has by no means enjoyed universal acceptance by party members in the Western democracies, particularly in those nations where communism is weak and in need of the psychological support of a powerful external ally. Such is the case in the United States, Denmark, West Germany, Austria and Portugal, where the parties adamantly denounce the Euro-Communist split and maintain loyalty to the Soviet Union. Without prospects of sharing in government, much less overthrowing it, what else can they do?

Actually, in Portugal, where the Communists are now led by Alvaro Cunhal, the closest thing in Western Europe to an old-line Stalinist, there were high hopes. In 1974, with the collapse of a long-term dictatorship, a variety of parties vied for control: Communists on one side, near-fascists on the other, with democratic socialists tightroping down the middle. It was a time for military coup and countercoup. The Communists seemed to have a real chance, but by accepting Soviet support and rejecting the developing ideas of Euro-Communism, their popularity quickly declined and the Socialists, Portugal's largest political party, have continued to maintain a shaky democracy between the extremes of left and right.

If the importance today of Euro-Communism is undeniable, there is no such consensus among political experts in assessing its implications. On the one hand, France's Jean-François Revel, author of *The Totalitarian Temptation,* refuses to regard it as anything more than the same old Communist wolf, dressed in lamb's clothing. Given a hand in government, he believes, the Communists will devour their meek socialist allies in the tradition of what took place throughout Eastern Europe following World War II, with the same result—democracy being cast aside by a totalitarian state.

Even if Revel is wrong, there is little doubt that the success of Euro-Communism would weaken the NATO alliance of Western nations. Yet the loudest lamentations are not coming from the United States, Britain, or West Germany, but from the Soviet Union, which, if it has learned to live with Western capitalism, sees Euro-Communism as a threat and a heresy. Russia is used to negotiating with the old "bourgeois" governments of Europe and does not want to face the uncertainties of a dramatic change. Worse, any emergent competitor for dominance in the Communist world would be a threat to Russia's position at the top. This fear is so acute that when Communists gathered in Moscow to celebrate the sixtieth anniversary of the Bolshevik revolution, Santiago Carrillo, Spain's outspoken advocate of Euro-Communism, was denied the right to speak. After all, if Western Europe can go its own way, what of those nations in the East, whose loyalty Russia has reason to suspect are based not so much upon belief in a common doctrine as upon the proximity of the mighty Soviet army?

Eastern Europe Eastern Europe is sometimes referred to as the "Communist bloc." It consists of East Germany, Poland, Czechoslovakia, Hungary, Yugoslavia, Bulgaria, Albania, and

Romania. On the whole, these countries lagged far behind the rest of Europe industrially before World War II. None were Communist, but all except Hungary had Communist parties. With the war and the German occupation, resistance developed. It prospered particularly in the mountainous regions of Yugoslavia. Unlike most of the other resistance groups, the Communist fighters were already organized and had growing support from outside. Their successes against the Germans were more spectacular. They were not encumbered so much by local interests. If the Germans burned down a town in response to an act of sabotage, the Communists would have that many more displaced and embittered recruits. Conversely, the prospering local citizen with love of town and country would hesitate before bringing down such havoc, and in many cases he did not act at all.

In this way domestic communism was doubly strengthened during the war years. With the Russian occupation of Eastern Europe during 1945, local Communist groups emerged from underground. Only in Yugoslavia and Albania had the local Communists displaced the German Army. This, along with strong nationalist feelings, had major implications for the future.

During the rosy glow of Allied victory, "Popular Democracies" were established throughout Eastern Europe. These democracies initially shared power among the bourgeois parties, the peasants, and the Communists. Gradually or rapidly, depending upon local circumstances, Soviet-backed Communists began to take over key positions in the law courts and among the police, so that by the spring of 1947 the coalition governments were giving way to complete Communist control. "Salami tactics" was what Hungary's Stalinist boss, Mátyás Rákosi, called this gradual slicing away of civil liberties.

Never was the issue one of workers and peasants battling the bourgeoisie. The only question, except in the case of Yugoslavia and Albania with their homegrown Communist governments already established, was the degree of cooperation with Moscow. With alternate threats of economic deprivation or the application of military force, if need be, it was Moscow that manipulated the situation from behind the scenes. While Stalin lived, the puppet states danced to his tune. With his death and subsequent vilification, many hardline Stalinists were dismissed or held up to ridicule. Unrest was felt throughout the entire Eastern European bloc, and in more than one case, as we will see later, revolution was attempted.

Nowhere did it succeed, yet nowhere has the near-monolithic structure of Eastern Europe been restored completely. Like a cracked ice floe, these countries continue to drift in the same current; yet they are drifting apart in the same way that the Western democracies, polarized around the United States after World War II, have increasingly become independent and learned to make their own decisions. Within this general context, the countries of Eastern Europe must be examined independently, for national characteristics, details of geography, episodes, and personalities have particularized them as individuals within the family of communism.

East Germany The DDR, or German Democratic Republic, is the only Eastern-bloc country born of World War II. Prewar Germany had had its Communists, but few survived the conflict. About the time Hitler, deep in his Berlin bunker, was putting a pistol into his mouth, Walter Ulbricht followed the Russian tanks into Germany from his exile in Moscow. This returning German was Stalin's disciple, and Ulbricht's original purpose was to aid the Soviet military authorities in their efforts to normalize civilian life in Germany. He arrived in devastated Berlin on May 2, 1945, and set about organizing an administration before the Western Allies could come and register complaints. At first, there was no sign of a Communist coup. In fact, Stalin must have been uncertain what course the future would take. The military occupation was regarded as temporary, and reunification with the Western two-thirds of the country was a possibility.

The eventual split, which began in earnest during the summer of 1948 with the Soviet land blockade of West Berlin, was as much a consequence as a cause of the growing cold war. That same autumn, East Germany's People's Council began drafting an East German Constitution and the German

Democratic Republic was proclaimed in 1949. But not until 1952 did Stalin commit East Germany to the people's democracy that he had initiated throughout the rest of Eastern Europe. Then the usual process was applied. A local Communist party took orders from Moscow, and there was final amalgamation with and absorption of the competitive socialist party. Then Walter Ulbricht, a good Stalinist and leader of the SED-Socialist United Party, took over.

Times were hard. While West Germany was being rebuilt by Marshall Plan aid, Russia was making good on her demands for reparations at the expense of East Germany. What remained of East German industry was packed off to the Soviet Union. No rebuilding took place. Young people fled the country. With the pathetic resources available, Ulbricht set about organizing a "command" economy based on the Soviet model. The worker was elevated and idealized so that it became easier for a worker's son to get to the university than for the son of a professor.

One day Adolf Hennecke, a coal miner of the heroic John Henry stamp, became a hated national hero for digging 6.4 cubic meters of coal in a Zwichau mine. This was nearly four times the daily norm, which in consequence was dramatically raised. Such episodes, plus overwork and inadequate pay, led to increasing unrest until, in the spring of 1953, a general workers' strike began and spread. Higher wages and free elections were demanded. It took Soviet tanks to put a final end to the outburst. But during the 1950s one-fifth of the native population of East Germany fled to the West. Curiously, it was this explosion of discontent that saved Ulbricht from being toppled by his lieutenants. Stalin had just died, and Ulbricht was a puritanical, doctrinaire Stalinist of the old school who had never defied the Kremlin in the days when his more idealistic colleagues were vanishing one by one.

Now, facing the workers' unrest, he defied Moscow's order for moderation and tried turning the Stalinist screws. If the dissent had subsided without Ulbricht's stern measures, Moscow would undoubtedly have supported his complaining subordinates. But such was the upheaval that Russia was obliged to give military support to Ulbricht's regime. When the trouble finally died down, he had weathered the storm and his erstwhile usurpers had been demoted. It must be said in Ulbricht's behalf that, though he emulated Stalin's ruthlessness, he was not equally merciless. His party purges were not accompanied by liquidation.

Though the Soviet tanks had nipped revolution in the bud, they could not otherwise help the floundering DDR. It took time, determination, and an ugly symbol of totalitarian repression to turn the trick. Just after midnight on Sunday, August 13, 1961, trucks and tanks rolled into Berlin and began unraveling barbed wire. Two days later came concrete for a city-wide wall. Thus was sealed an escape hatch through which 160,000 East Berliners had fled the city in a period of seven months. According to Ulbricht, the wall was designed to repel "Western kidnappers and agitators." But clearly it had the purpose of keeping people in, not out. And it worked—far better than Ulbricht had anticipated. Not only did it keep people in; it destroyed hope for a better life outside. It forced East Germans to resign themselves to make the best of a bad situation, and they got to work.

The result has been an economic miracle. Of course, conditions in East Germany do not compare with the flashy affluence of West Germany, which had an industrial tradition to begin with, as well as United States' aid to repair war damage. But the DDR has become in a few short years the eighth largest industrial power in the world. People live comfortably there, if not luxuriously. Nonessentials remain terribly expensive. But buying a television set ten years ago meant waiting two years for it to arrive at the store, at which point one had to pedal it home resting precariously on the handlebars of a bicycle. Now a technician will bring the set and install it on the day of purchase. In 1965, refrigerators were nine months back-ordered. Today they come immediately, with an eight-day trial period. Nowhere in the Eastern Soviet bloc is the living standard as high as in East Germany. For those who can afford them, there are even imported luxuries, with Scotch available at 36 dollars a bottle, and Volkswagen Rabbits being snapped up at 13,000 dollars per car in 1978.

Progress is the result of not only a different attitude but

of a change in economic approach. Under the old doctrinal command economy, the measure of success was quota, not profit. Results were often ludicrous, if not disastrous. A pajama-factory manager with a quota to fill but with insufficient allocation of fabric would progressively shorten the pants of the pajamas. A popular joke had two Chinese engineers visiting an East German factory and expressing admiration for what was produced there. "Very good, comrades—parts for elevators. We don't have them yet." Then, going too far, the Chinese ask, "What parts are they?" and receive the answer, "Signs reading 'Out of Order'."

All that began to change under the direction of Dr. Günter Mittag, tsar of East German industry. The DDR has gone further that its Soviet patron in shifting over to a decentralized system based on profit, even though the profit motive remains by definition at the root of all capitalist evils. Pure capitalism is not in the works. But a socialized network called the Vereinigungen Volkseigener Betriebe (Association of People's Owned Enterprises) covers many branches of manufacturing and distribution. In the more specialized areas, there still remains much private industry. Among the trades, about half of the shoemakers, watchmakers, plasterers, and electricians have joined cooperatives that offer a flat salary. At the price of losing independence, security is offered with the profits above salary being banked and given out as a dividend at the end of the year.

In the retail field, state-owned supermarkets are replacing the corner grocer simply because of convenience. In one area there has been backtracking toward more private ownership. When the state took over restaurants, cafés, and bars, the cherished German *Gemütlichkeit*—warm good cheer—went out of the establishments, and they were not patronized. Where the individual and the private touch serve the best interest of the state, it is no longer interfered with simply to please Marx or Lenin. The East Germans are too hardheaded and practical to let theory interfere with success—so long as they do not feel the muzzle of a Russian gun at their backs.

To justify the "Democratic" in their official masthead, the DDR has faithfully held elections, each one preceded by massive rallies and ardent speeches. Until 1965, results were assured since the ballot carried only one slate of Communist candidates. Voters had to fill out this ballot under official scrutiny. About the only possibility for a negative response was to boycott the affair. This could not hurt the candidates, but it might well imperil the voter's future. Then, in 1965, the list of candidates began to exceed the number of vacancies by about 20 percent. For example, for twenty available offices there would be twenty-four names. However, the names at the top were preferred. And the last four would not be elected even though their votes exceeded any of the first twenty unless the twenty received less than 50 percent of the votes. A small concession to democracy, admittedly. It has done very little to shake up the party structure, but it has done a great deal to put the candidates on their mettle. A defeat, a slight possibility for a preferred candidate, would be ruinously humiliating. Even a narrow margin of victory will put a dark cloud over that man's political future, and so campaigns are conducted with more zeal than before.

East Germany today is the most prosperous and, after Bulgaria, the most loyal of Russian satellites. With a population of Prussian background, accustomed to authoritarian leadership, totalitarian socialism has worked well. Although many may chafe under the regime, almost all take pride in the results of their new socialized economic system. Prospects become ever brighter. The DDR is planning for the future with one of the best and most costly school systems in Europe. Seventy percent of her young people receive ten or more years of education compared to only 30 percent in West Germany.

Of course, the doctrinaire viewpoint is twisted. History is seen as the class struggle of the oppressed versus the exploiter, and the Roman gladiator Spartacus gets more attention than Christianity in a study of ancient Rome. The history of medieval and Renaissance Europe is presented as nothing but peasants rising up against their feudal lords. Not all of this is swallowed whole by an increasingly sophisticated student body, who learn the need to mimic but not necessarily to believe. Technically, in science and mathematics, preparation is excellent, and a resurgent DDR is moving smoothly into the computer age.

But a heavy price is paid. The DDR is a dull and oppressive society, its population of 17,096,000 dominated by 2 million energetic Communists who are omnipresent in even the smallest village. Only carefully selected foreign books can be found in libraries, and woe betide the student who speaks up in protest. Recently a foreign exchange student received a seven-year jail sentence for "provocative criticism endangering the state." In fact, during a heated student debate, he had insisted that, without the presence of twenty Soviet divisions in the DDR, the regime could not be maintained. Foolhardy to speak out so candidly, but the implications of the punishment are staggering.

There are other techniques for dealing with internal dissent. In 1976 a socially critical folk singer, Wolf Biermann, who went on a Western concert tour, was told not to return. The following year Jurek Becker, a prominent writer, was not allowed to publish his current manuscript. He is now in the West. Many dissenting artists have been kicked out. In Communist theory an independent artist is, after all, something of a freak, and social parasite at best. They are the lucky ones. Those with professional training are denied the right to leave. In fact, even to make such an application is grounds for the courts to charge them with "incitement hostile to the state," which in turn means jail and the likelihood of a degrading menial job thereafter. To mediate this harsh situation it has become common practice for West Germany to "buy out" East German political prisoners in exchange for consumer goods which are enjoyed by party members.

What of the future? For years there was the expectation that Germany would be reunified. As the years went by it was said, not entirely in jest, that shopkeepers were putting up signs, "East and West German spoken here." In 1974 the United States officially acknowledged the rift by establishing diplomatic relations with the DDR. An exchange of ambassadors followed. In 1975 the existence of two Germanies was confirmed at the Helsinki conference on security and cooperation. So the break with one greater Germany of the past seems complete. What of a break with the earlier days of the Communist regime? Spokesman and pillar for the old ways was Walter Ulbricht. At 77 he stepped down and his lieutenant, Erich Honecker, took over.

Ulbricht was in control longer than Hitler, and the state made undeniable economic progress under him. His successor is a reasonable facsimile, moving in the same firm, conservative, and essentially unimaginative direction. But there is a pragmatic younger generation hopeful of taking over. They are not revolutionaries, for they are confident of their achievements within their socialist system. But many have wearied of the dogmatic restraints of strict Marxism. To the new intelligentsia of the DDR, both within and outside the party, the old rote phraseology that has served their elders demands editing. And whatever their pride of accomplishment, few can entirely forget the 856 miles (1,370 km) of concrete slabs, bricked-up buildings, watchtowers, land mines, and yapping dogs that remain a tangible symbol of man's inhumanity to man. Some sort of change cannot be kept out forever.

Economically, then, East Germany has made a success of communism. From an initial adherence to the Soviet model, a more pragmatic spirit has evolved and is drifting away from the rigid social and economic patterns of the past. Whether democratic and humanistic progress can be kept out by an aging regime remains to be seen. Time, in the long run, would seem to be against it, though East Germany is a land accustomed to regimentation.

Russia's other European satellites appear to fall into two groups: in the north, the more Western-oriented trio of Poland, Czechoslovakia, and Hungary; in the south, the more remote area often referred to as the Balkans, including Bulgaria and Romania, and two Communist countries outside the Russian orbit, Albania and Yugoslavia. Beyond the obvious element of geographical location, though, the division has little merit. Physical proximity or remoteness from direct Russian military supervision naturally has been a factor in shaping the policies of these nations. But each has had its own unique history and evolution, and so we will consider them one by one, beginning with the three Central European countries.

Poland Geography cannot be ignored in the case of Russia's most northern satellite. Poland has had the historical misfortune of occupying ground between two strong, agressive powers—the Teutonic and the Russian. Repeatedly over the centuries the land has been occupied by both Germany and Russia, and it was divided between Prussia, Russia, and Austria from the end of the eighteenth century until 1919, when it became an independent country. In recent times the aggressive powers have worn the guise of two expansionist ideologies, nazism and communism. Poland was Hitler's first target in World War II, and Stalin was also quick to take a slice of the pie. Before Russia had time to digest her section, Hitler seized all of the rest of Poland.

Throughout the war, the Polish government existed in exile, directing resistance from London. This resistance was intense and free of Communist infiltration, but it was removed from the homeland. On Polish soil, Hitler unwittingly prepared the way for communism. With the beginning of the Nazi withdrawal, Polish resistance rose openly. The Nazis lingered long enough to destroy the flower of Polish patriotism. This bloodletting was achieved with the cynical cooperation of Moscow, which withheld its attack until Polish resistance had bled to death.

By the end of the war, the Polish people were decimated. The only source of power belonged to the Russian occupiers, who began their occupation by providing a committee of national liberation. By 1947, under a new "proletarian" constitution, the country had come under tight Soviet control. Heavy industry was nationalized along with most of the medium industry, wholesale activities, and retail trades. Not until the airing of Stalin's transgressions did opposition once more grow in Poland. In June of 1956, workers at the Zispo locomotive works began chanting, "We want bread." Riots ensued. Over fifty people were killed, but the rebellion never took as drastic a form as it did elsewhere that year. And it was quelled by concessions, with no need for Russia's physical interference. These bread strikes ushered in a period called "Golden October" under a new party secretary, Wladyslaw Gomulka. He had been imprisoned during the Stalinist era, and he arrived with the promise of dramatic reform. He kept the Soviet Army out by persuading Khrushchev that his policies would not deviate. This promise was sincere, for if he distrusted Russia, he hated Germany, and the Russian alliance made for security against the ingrained fear of a Teutonic foe.

The factors that make for individuality in Polish communism are many. Among the most obvious are Poland's Western outlook and traditional distrust of Russia, historically rooted in countless wars. Russia's cooperation with Hitler before World War II eradicated any possible illusions. There is more gloom than amusement in the joke that goes, "Comrades, for every boxcar load of meat we ship to Russia, we get a boxcar load of shoes . . . for repair."

The key to Poland's resistance is the Catholic church, too strong to be uprooted. Over 90 percent of the population of the country are practicing Catholics. Most Polish Communist party members are nominal Catholics despite the theoretical incompatability of the two. And since 1957 religious instruction has been given in schools.

The present situation in Poland is by no means stabilized. Thus far, unrest has been channeled into strikes rather than resulting in revolution. Gomulka dismantled some collective farms and ostensibly diminished the secret police, but, under the label of eliminating political reaction, he sanctioned persecution of Poland's Jewish population. The hounding out of the country of these last few survivors of Hitler's death camps brought with it a revival of the secret police. Subsequently, an economic failure in 1970 led to a rise in the price of food and other necessities, with a corresponding drop in luxury prices. Many Poles interpreted this policy as "Let them eat refrigerators," and at the Gdansk shipyard workers attacked police with bicycle chains. Disturbances spread. Signs went up, "We are workers, not hooligans." Under pressure, Gomulka abdicated.

Edward Gierek became the new First Secretary. In 1974 at

the thirtieth-anniversary celebration of the People's Republic he could proudly point to production up 20 times since before World War II. The following year he received a visit from President Gerald Ford. Trade with the United States and other Western nations has soared. President Jimmy Carter paid his respects during Christmas week of 1977, and relations seemed even more cordial. But despite his international successes, Gierek must face the same domestic situation which led to his predecessor's fall—riots over sharply increased food prices. Waiting on shopping lines has become such a national pastime that the otherwise unemployed hire themselves out as substitutes. In 1976 when bloody riots threatened, the government yielded and prices were rolled back. At the moment Gierek seems comfortably in the saddle but economic problems persist and the horse he is riding is no docile beast of the East German sort. With its independently minded workers and strong Catholic church, Gierek must share his power or run the risk of being thrown down.

Czechoslovakia Poland's southern neighbor, Czechoslovakia, was also used to Western ways before World War II. Industrialized, educated, and prosperous, the country's Communists were a respectable minority party before the war. Hitler seized Czechoslovakia more by threat than violence, and the later ravages of defeat did not touch it. However, the "liberating" Soviet Army was welcomed as a guarantee against Germany's age-old policy of *Drang nach Osten* ("push to the East"). The Nazi puppet government was overripe for the ax, and in 1946 Communists gained 38 percent of the vote. However, as the impact of the war faded, the popularity of Communist protection also diminished. The tide threatened to turn entirely in 1947 when Marshall Plan aid was offered, and the Communists had to work fast. Workers were armed and mass demonstrations organized. On February 25, 1948, without benefit of overt Soviet intervention, a coup took place. By summer President Eduard Beneš had resigned, but Jan Masaryk refused to surrender his post at the foreign office. He was found dead beneath his window. A Communist deputy succeeded him. Under the Communists a dismal and unimaginative rule was imposed, and Czech wealth and industrial know-how were drained to Russia.

In spite of the harassment of Czechoslovak intellectuals, the cultural life in Czechoslovakia eventually revived. It even intoxicated party boss Alexander Dubček, who began relaxing press controls and demoting hard-line Stalinists. Unlike Gomulka in Poland, he paid little heed to Russian rumblings. While Dubček's moves were a small threat to communism, they did question Moscow's dominant position. On August 20, 1968, Party Secretary Breznev took action. For the sake of appearance, he heard a cry of help from the Czech Communist party. Though Brezhnev alone heard this appeal, Soviet, East German, Polish, Hungarian and Bulgarian troops went to the rescue. The Czechs awoke from dreaming to the rumble of Russian tanks. "Lenin, wake up! Brezhnev has gone mad!" appeared on many walls. Overwhelmed virtually without a fight, Dubček was drummed out of his official position, but not murdered. Censorship and the old totalitarian ways returned, under the leadership of Gustav Husak. Unrest continues. In 1976 Husak, a relative moderate within the context of Soviet communism, found himself beset on the one hand by a clique of hard-line Communists and on the other by the old leadership deposed in 1968.

Without this interference from outside, Czechoslovakia would be on the way to being an independent Communist state. But the change had come too fast. The official government is now strictly subservient to Russian dictates. Below this crust the intellectuals, the students, and the discontented ones remain. As long as Chekhov's play *The Three Sisters* ran, the loudest applause was bestowed upon an actor watching the departure of soldiers from a small Russian town. He said only, "They left." But open dissent is not tolerated. Intellectuals who tried to implement the Helsinki accords have been persecuted. In 1976 two groups of rock musicians, The Plastic People of the Universe and DG307, were jailed for singing antisocialist songs. The future can never be guessed, but of the past and the present this much can be said: of all the Eastern European countries under communism, the doctrine's application is least appropriate in Czechoslovakia, for communism's virtues lie in upgrading backward, undereducated countries; its vices, in restricting the individual. Czechoslovakia—the one Eastern European country with a democratic tradition and an industrialized economy—had nothing to gain from communism.

Hungary Hungary is thought of in the framework of her bloody revolt against communism in 1956, but her struggle for freedom had begun long before that. Dominated for centuries by the Ottoman Empire and by the Hapsburgs of Austria, Hungary became, in 1867, a member of the dual Austro-Hungarian monarchy, and, as such, it took part in World War I, losing much territory to Romania, Yugoslavia, and Czechoslovakia. In the hopes of getting some land back, Hungary joined Hitler: another bad choice, which left the country finally at Stalin's mercy. Under Stalin's deputy, Mátyás Rákosi, the takeover was thorough and harsh. Radical industrialization and collectivization took place. With Stalin's death, repercussions in Hungary were more violent than elsewhere, since a regime so closely associated with his policies had to be discredited.

With peasants assaulting collectivism and intellectuals demanding free expression, Imre Nagy took over the de-Stalinized government, granted concessions, and dreamed of drastic reforms. He was forced out of office in 1955. But by the early autumn of 1956 the pendulum of reform had swung out of the government's control. Students milled in the streets. Industrial workers met, demanding free trade unions. Then political police fired into a crowd. Fighting spread, and the Hungarian Army went over to the "freedom fighters." By the end of October, victory was close at hand, Nagy was reinstated, and the new government appealed to the United Nations for support. Their timing was unlucky. France and Britain had invaded Egypt in a blatant show of imperialism during the Suez crisis. Encouraged by this example and fearing a collapse of its own "colonial empire," Russia moved into Hungary with five thousand tanks. Thirty-five thousand Hungarians died in the hopeless fight while the world watched. Two hundred thousand fled to the West, and then the struggle was over.

With the champions of independence dead, imprisoned, or

self-exiled, communism was oppressively reinstated. At this point, the country seemed doomed to the strictest form of totalitarian communism as a mere Russian puppet, manipulated by Moscow's hired hand, Janos Kádár. Time has somewhat modified this gloomy judgment, largely because of Kádár himself, who has proved to be no commonplace quisling. Despite strict control of the press, suppression of intellectual expression, and the presence of the Soviet Army, the outcome has been what some Hungarians call goulash communism. Shops are crammed with Western goods, and Count Basie has paid a visit. On television forums, government officials can be questioned by telephone, and some of the dreams of the 1956 revolt seem to be coming true. Collective farms have been granted more autonomy, and, as with other Eastern-bloc nations, factories have moved from the old command economy to a program allowing sensitivity to Westernized free-market factors. Industrial development and planning have been decentralized, and priorities have been reorganized to emphasize agriculture along with heavy industry. The economy has kept on schedule and increasing food prices have been matched by larger paychecks.

All this has come about subject to one absolute limitation. In Kádár's words, "It is impossible to be a Communist and at the same time anti-Soviet." Principally, this means subservience to Russian foreign policy. Kádár's only deviations thus far have been in the direction of excessive zeal, for example, in his offer of volunteers to North Vietnam. For the time being, then, it seems that Hungary's foreign policy will mirror Moscow's. Domestically, the quiet revolution is likely to progress slowly within the limitations set by a vigilantly totalitarian government.

The Balkans The Balkans are a largely mountainous cluster of countries, most of which are now Communist, that conjure up gypsies and guitar music. They are relatively foreign and remote, lost between East and West. Throughout history, this has been an area of perpetual political upheaval that in recent times has tempted great powers. Here modern states have been built out of the disintegrating Ottoman Empire. And the Balkan geographical divisions do not completely reflect the diverse cultures and ethnic minorities of the area. Though these nations have shared the ordeal of foreign overlordship, none feels comfortable with the others. Yugoslavia stands independent. Bulgaria remains loyal to Russia. Albania has become the enemy of Russia and until the death of Mao the close ally of China, a bond which has weakened since the Chinese leader's death. Romania, the so-called Latin Island in the Slavic sea, craves Western culture and seems on the verge of quietly obtaining it.

Greece and European Turkey are also in the Balkans; neither has a firmly democratic government, but both are anticommunist and allied with the West. Only a fragment of Turkey occupies the Balkan peninsula, where it borders Bulgaria. To the East, beyond the Dardanelles, its longer and more sensitive Asian frontier faces the Soviet Union. These two have been enemies since the eighteenth century, and Russia's conversion to communism has done nothing to lessen Turkish distrust.

Though the Soviet Union would dearly love to command the strategic area that Turkey occupies, it is not likely to do so. Turkey's noninvolvement in World War II made Communist guerrilla subversion impractical, and unswerving Turkish vigilance against all things Russian has not permitted Moscow to get its foot in the door. Recently, Turkey has been experimenting with Western-style democracy, but the real power in the country remains with the military. The resulting instability makes for political unrest, but at the moment communism seems a very unpropitious direction for that discontent to take.

Greece, until recently, was ruled by soldiers, though past events created a setting similar to that of her Communist neighbors. Resistance to Germany divided right and left as it did in the other Balkan countries with the exception of Bulgaria and Romania, which took the German side. The Communist guerrillas prevailed in Greece before the war ended and would undoubtedly have controlled the country afterward had not Churchill ordered the landing of British troops at Piraeus. Not only was Greece far from the Russian frontier; it alone had emotional importance for the Western Allies as the democratic cradle of civilization. When the British finally exhausted themselves in the attempt to preserve Greece for the West, the United States stepped in with massive aid. When Yugoslavia became involved with Russia, the Greek frontier was closed to Communist infiltration. By 1949 Greece had been saved from communism. Civilian government, after a period of seven years of military dictatorship, was restored in 1974. In July, Konstantinos Karamanlis became prime minister and founded the New Democratic party. With this return of freedom, Communist parties became legal for the first time since 1949, and there are three of them: the Communist Party of the Exterior, which is subsidized by Russia and follows the Moscow line; the independent Communist Party of the Interior; finally, the United Democratic left, a nationalistic Marxist group. There is little love lost between the three, and none is politically strong.

Otherwise, throughout the Balkan peninsula communism was methodically successful after World War II. Where the governments had allied themselves with Hitler or been forced into humiliating capitulation, they were easy prey to Communist subversion. Totalitarian regimes were instituted, shaken and then modified along more pragmatic lines after Stalin's denunciation. About more than this, it is hard to generalize, and it is the differences in these countries rather than the similarities that deserve exploration.

Yugoslavia Though Communist, Yugoslavia and Albania stand apart from Russia's Balkan satellites. In many ways, Albania is a negative image of Yugoslavia; in Khrushchev's scornful words Albania is "a place for goats." But Yugoslavia has unequaled importance as far as the development of world communism is concerned. As a matter of geographic convenience and in the hope several small quarrelsome countries could be lumped into one more manageable unit, Yugoslavia was created after World War I by lumping together Serbia and Montenegro with former Austro-Hungarian lands of the South Slavs. The result was unworkable. Hostile Serbs, Croats, Catholics, Muslims, and Greek Orthodox glared at one another under the rule of Serbian kings. In 1941 the army ousted the pro-German regency with the cry, "Better war than the pact," referring to a nonaggression pact that had been signed with Germany. The price of opposition to the pact was blood. Official resistance was crushed by the Germans in a week. Though elements of the army kept together under the right-wing leadership of Draža Mihajlović, his following was limited.

By 1943, the Communists were the only effective force in Yugoslavia still resisting the Nazis. They had begun as 12,000 men, but only 3,000 of this nucleus survived the war. Their slogan was "Brotherhood and unity for all Yugoslavs." And their appeal was limited to no single ethnic or religious group. Despite terrible casualties at the hands of the Germans, by the war's end their fighting force had grown to 140,000. Their leader, Josip Broz, known today as Marshal Tito, emerged a shining national hero.

During World War I, Tito had served in the Austro-Hungarian army. Taken prisoner, he had been trained as a Communist in Russia, and he returned to head the party in Yugoslavia as early as 1937. During the war he had won his own battles and the final victory without Stalin's help. Thereafter, Tito went ahead to found the Federal People's Republic of Yugoslavia, a Communist state that he fully expected would outstrip Soviet accomplishments. Russia was delighted. More Stalinist than Stalin, Yugoslavia thumbed its nose at the United States and shot down her airplanes. Police terror reigned. Collective farms were set up, and complete faith in Marxist doctrine gave over the economy to heavy industry with no concern for the consumer.

The Marxist romance between Yugoslavia and Russia did not last long. Stalin was used to having his suggestions carried out to the letter, but Tito, too, was a hard fighter of the old school. In a letter to Stalin he said that no matter how much he loved the land of socialism, meaning Russia, he could not love his own country less. To Stalin, the implication of this honest patriotism was heresy. He began proclaiming "Titoism" as the disease of "National Communism." Tito retracted nothing.

In Yugoslavia, June 28 is a day full of portent. It is not only Saint Vitus' Day, a national saint's day, but also the anniversary of "The Field of Blackbirds" when, in 1389, Turkey had extinguished Serbian independence. More important still, it was the occasion in 1914 for a Bosnian youth to kill Archduke Franz Ferdinand, thereby precipitating World War I. On this date, June 28, 1948, came the announcement that Yugoslavia was expelled from the Cominform. Invasion was anticipated.

Yugoslavia was helped by geographical remoteness from Russia as well as by her reputation as a fighter, and Soviet response was limited to an economic blockade. Tito was forced to look Westward for aid. While doing so, he began to rethink his political philosophy. "We are searching for our way," he said. With Stalin's passing, Khrushchev tried to make amends. He blamed the quarrel on Stalin, saying, "Our countries are linked by ties of long brotherly friendship and joint struggle." In so doing, he acknowledged a kind of independence on the part of Yugoslavia, a new posture that did not go unnoticed in the other Eastern satellites.

Regardless of this rapprochement with Russia, Yugoslavia had found its own way by this time, and that way will probably always be referred to as "Titoism." In agriculture, Tito was afflicted after the war with the Soviet tractor obsession. One must free labor for industry. In Marxian terms, the goal had been to destroy the pillar of the old society, "the peasant," and replace him with the salaried farmer. By 1948, collectivism was going full blast, but its first five years were a disaster. In 1953, the ex-peasants were told they might leave the collectives. They left, preferring to start again from scratch.

Heavy industry has always been the Marxist key, and Tito tried at first to fit it to the Yugoslav lock. He tried so zealously that he recruited workers from the farms until there were great pools of industrial unemployed. When rejection by the Cominform forced him to look to foreign markets, he accepted the doctrine of supply and demand in order to survive. Workers were given new incentives such as shares in their factory's profits, and they were allowed workers' councils with their own elected leadership.

Today Yugoslavian borders have been opened to easy coming and going, and there is an air of prosperity in the land. One has the inclination to reflect upon the plucky little country that told the USSR where to get off, the perfect example of freedom-loving patriotism. That independent stature is fine as far as it goes, but politically Yugoslavia remains a one-party totalitarian state. The party itself is free internationally to go its own way. It can condemn Communist China or Russia as it chooses. It was more moderate than most Communist nations in attacking the United States on its Vietnam activities. But let a writer, even a good friend of Tito's such as Milovan Djilas, criticize the Communist society in writing and propose the introduction of a multiparty government, and that man risks jail for defaming Yugoslavia's Communist society and fomenting national hatred. Mihajlo Mihajlov is another important writer imprisoned for three and a half years by Tito. The Yugoslav citizen has certain freedoms, but he does not live in an entirely free society.

What follows Titoism? The question is an important one, for Yugoslavia's president-for-life, though as defiant as ever, is 85 years old. In 1977 there were rumors that his 54-year-old wife Jovanka Broz-Tito was plotting with military officers against him. Nothing has come of that, and his great personal magnetism keeps the crowds chanting, "Tito is ours, we are Tito's", and the children singing, "Tito, Tito, little white flower, beloved by all the youth." Presently he must step down. Will old ethnic rivalries then be renewed and tear the country apart as they have before? Probably not. Already Tito has proposed for the future a "collective presidency" of the two or three best men, one from each of the nation's republics. Already much of the administration and detail is in other hands. If these men can work together, harmonizing the interests of the groups they represent, then Yugoslavia would seem to have a bright and prosperous future.

Bulgaria There remain three Balkan nations—Bulgaria, Albania, and Romania—to be touched on, and all three have uncertain prospects. They are all small, unlikely to shake the world. To begin with Bulgaria: it is poor and primitive and too seasick from being a pawn in international struggles to want to rock the boat. Even before the advent of Soviet communism, Bulgaria had been an appendage of tsarist Russia, which she accepted as a bodyguard against Turkey on the one side and old Western foes on the other. The bloodletting of World War I left the small country battered, dazed, worse off than before. Discontent smouldered. Alexander Stambuliski, leader of the leftist-leaning Agrarian party, became premier. He initiated enlightened reforms, only to be seized in 1923 by members of a fascist group, the International Macedonian Revolutionary Organization (IMRO). He was made to dig his own grave. Then his right arm, which had tried to curb IMRO, was hacked off before he was murdered. Terror bred counter-terror throughout the following years. In 1941 Nazi troops invaded. Bulgaria was forced to declare war on England and France, though she refused to do so in regard to her old patron, Russia. Once the Germans retreated in the summer of 1944, Bulgaria opened peace talks with Great Britain and the United States and on September 3 formed a pro-Western government. This was too much for Stalin, who for the first time declared war on Bulgaria and sent in troops. Bulgaria has been a Soviet pawn ever since—with Todor Zhivkov, who became a loyal premier in 1962, still chairman of the state council. At times, a Bulgarian will joke about Russia. During the Chinese-Indian border dispute, both sides were using Russian arms, and it was said in Bulgaria that for this reason the war would go on forever, since nobody could win with Soviet weapons. A mild joke, but seldom whispered in official Bulgarian circles where one can be jailed for up to five years for simply leading "an idle, parasitic way of life."

Albania Khrushchev was undoubtedly correct when he said that there are more goats than people in the Albanian population. An Albanian takes pride in the statement that "God must love Albania since it has changed so little since the Creation." During the war, resistance to Italian and German invaders polarized left and right as it did in Yugoslavia. Characteristically, the Communists prevailed. Fearing her neighbor, Yugoslavia, more than the remote Soviet Union, Albania started out as Russia's slavish disciple. However, when Tito and Khrushchev began their courtship, Albania's boss, Enver Hoxha, a former schoolteacher and guerrilla leader, protested. He feared that his country might become a wedding present to Marshal Tito. On one occasion he complained to Khrushchev that the Soviet rats were being better fed than his people, to which the Russian leader replied, "You have emptied a pail of manure on my head." Until this time, China had meant very little to Albania, but with the Sino-Soviet split, Albania could find some comfort in supporting Chinese policy. Where they had once addressed Tito with "We and the Russians, 200 million," now it was "We and the Chinese, 650 million."

Albania has attempted to solve severe ethnic and religious unrest by means of murder and forced emigration and has effected a strong program of collectivization in both industry and land. Recently, the tumult and the shouting have died down. Yugoslavia seems content without her neighbor's goats, and a long-term bond between Albania and China, apart from a means of jabbing Russia in the ribs, seems hardly likely. In 1976 Hoxha presented a new constitution that abolished private property, made the sexes legally equal, and eliminated religious foundations. As a counterweight to this hard-line approach, a trickle of tourists have at last been allowed into the country. Scandinavian students have begun a summer invasion that may in time work more changes than Tito's tanks, for Albania is a land poised between the sixteenth and the twentieth centuries.

Romania Lastly there is Rumania, calling itself in recent years Romania. There is some significance behind this one-letter alteration in the country's name, which came about officially in 1966. That period brought about an easing of civil restraints and new independence in foreign policy to Romania, shown for example in its failure to condemn Israel as did the other members of the Warsaw Pact, a mutual defense treaty signed by the Soviet-bloc European Communist countries in 1955. The changing of Romania's name is a reflection not only of nationalist assertion but of a claim to a Roman background. At one time, the country was conquered and settled by Romans. The ethnic strain is still present so that the Romanians can claim some connection with Latin Europe.

Before the Romanians became involved in World War II, Russia had grabbed off a large chunk of Romanian real estate called Bessarabia. With Hitler's help, the Romanians took it back. By 1944, however, the handwriting was on the wall. The old profascist government collapsed, and backed by Soviet tanks, communism took its place. At first Romania stepped reluctantly into line and went about building up its economy with the usual concentration on industry. Until this time, though rich in oil, the country had been little industrialized. Rapid growth was facilitated by the lack of old equipment.

The economy leapt ahead until 1962, when to counter Western Europe's Common Market, Moscow revised its own plan, Comecon, to accomodate non-European membership. In Russia's view, the economic progress of the entire Communist camp lay in the coordination of production, a kind of socialist division of labor. At the same time, Russia often took what it wanted from satellite countries, with no repayment. Under Comecon, Romania was to become the source of raw material for the Communist states. From the beginning Romania balked, preferring the theory that each Communist nation should develop its own economy. Naturally, as this made for independence and competition, it went counter to Russia's desire to dominate the entire group of countries. For the first time, largely thanks to Romania's adamant stand, Russia was forced to abandon a major policy line.

For success, of course, outside trade is necessary, and Romania has never been loath to look to the West. Under Communist party boss Nicolae Ceausescu, head of the party since 1965, Romania has walked a tightrope. The summer of 1968 was one of near disaster. Less outspoken in its innovations, Romania had gone as far or farther toward independence than Czechoslovakia. At that time, the so-called Brezhnev Doctrine, justifying the invasion of Czechoslovakia and presumably any other state where the Communist system was endangered, was formulated. Romania protested, but kept its voice low, fearing the worst. Soviet troops did not appear, and Romania was left to go its way.

Since then, Romania has progressed independently and rapidly, with an annual growth rate far exceeding that of any of its neighbors. This obsession with pumping the bulk of the national income back into industrial development has of course caused domestic hardships and in the summer of 1977 resulted in massive protests, particularly on the part of the miners in the Jiu Valley. Government officials were seized and mine entrances blocked while the miners demanded better food, more consumer goods, improved housing, and pensions. Concessions were announced and then the troops moved in, with the leaders of the protest so thoroughly purged that by December 1977, President Ceausescu could call for eight more years of austerity to lift the country into the ranks of the developed nations.

On the side of independence, President Ceausescu has traveled widely, visiting Washington, D.C., in 1973 and 1975, as well as Peking. Romanian universities have been granted increasing autonomy and have sent the first delegation from a Communist nation to visit the United States and observe its space program. President Ceausescu has dared to speak favorably of Euro-Communism, and in 1976 defined proletarian internationalism as "full equality and comradely mutual assistance among all socialist countries." Mindful of his limitations, Ceausescu has affronted the Soviet Union only in the area of foreign policy. Domestically he has maintained a severely one-party system with strict controls on intellectual expression. A sad example of the latter was the seizure in December of 1977 of the cream of Bucharest's private art collections. These collections had already been deeded to the Romanian government on the condition that they remain on public display in the buildings where they had been collected. Romania's National Gallery already was overstocked but evidently with the objective of closing down small havens of imagination, their contents were seized and stored helter-skelter in the damp basements of the Palace of Culture and in the attics of the downtown National Museum, to be enjoyed exclusively by rats. But so long as Ceausescu does not overly offend his Soviet patrons and the economy continues to move upward, he can depend on holding the reins for some time to come.

To sum up briefly on the Eastern European Communist bloc: in all these countries, communism was established as a major force as a result of World War II—whereas formerly communism had been represented by minority parties only. Once instituted, communism adhered for a time to the absolute Marxist-Stalinist mold. Industrial growth was emphasized, usually with some success, particularly before the classic demand economy gave way to a more pragmatic market economy. In all cases, the firm adherence to older principles received a jolt with Stalin's death and subsequent denunciation. At this time it became clear that the dogmatism of the past had not permitted progress in the Eastern European countries. In a few cases, notably Hungary, the reaction went too far, resulting in abortive revolt and harsh consequences. But even in Hungary, a slow drift toward leniency has been renewed, and there has been a certain extension of freedom, particularly in the completely private sector. Where political criticism is concerned, all the governments of Eastern Europe have remained harsh. All remain one-party, totalitarian Communist, in part through fear of Russia. Most remain subservient to Russia in the international field, the exceptions being Yugoslavia, Albania, and Romania, where communism has become strongly nationalistic. Yugoslavia, in particular, is an example that Communist states of the future are likely to follow.

China, the Eastern Colossus

Massed red banners, echoing loudspeakers, gigantic posters of Chairman Mao Tse-tung—an Orwellian caricature not quite real—the red horde, as genuine and uncontrollably dangerous as nitroglycerin. These were for years and to an extent still are the Western stereotypes of the People's Republic of China. To the Soviet leaders, the pictures are not very different: arrogant, ungrateful upstart; perverter of Marx and Lenin; destroyer of Communist world unity; resurgent nightmare of the Mongol scourge. How did the moribund starved dragon of the opium dream revive so terrifyingly in fifty years? The answer is, of course, communism, creating with austere and selfless dedication what emperors for eons past seldom could: a single-minded purpose felt right down to the lowliest rice-paddy peasant. The facts are indisputable. The fair questions are: How? At what price? And most pressing, to what end?

No nation on Earth has stretching behind it such a long, continuous history as China. The Shang dynasty can be traced back to before 1700 B.C. As one dynasty declined, another rose to replace it. Art and literature reached a high point under the Ming emperors, accompanied by a dangerous contempt for the surrounding barbarian world, a contempt that persevered and grew with the Manchus from 1644 to 1912. Until about 1750, because of famine and disease China maintained a relatively small and manageable population of about one hundred million people. Then, with new medicines and drought-resistant crops, the number of people tripled within fifty years. The Manchus began to lose control of the situation. They arrogantly ignored industrial change in the "barbarian world," and they were helpless when British traders, bent on economic exploitation, began bringing opium into China. At first it was a trickle, then a debilitating flood. Junks armed with archers were no match for Western gunboats. Britain first, then other nations took over the exploitation of China and set in motion the biggest drug problem the world has ever known. As the emperors lost stature, the inevitable contagion of Western ways bred revolutionary ideas and encouraged powerful warlords to independent conduct.

The Kuomintang Finally, in 1911, a bomb cached in a revolutionary headquarters accidentally exploded. Manchu officials, on behalf of the boy emperor, Hsüan-t'ung, began making arrests. Rebels fought back, and in Denver, Colorado, a thirty-four-year-old Chinese doctor who had been raising funds for a Chinese revolution heard the news and headed home. Sun Yat-sen arrived in Shanghai on Christmas Day. By then all of South China was in flames. Within a year, he would emerge as leader of the Kuomintang, "the National People's party," and he would be the first president of the Republic of China. The republic was more of a phantom than a reality. Although the powerful General Yüan Shih-k'ai was president of the republic for a short period, he perverted the aims of the revolution. After his death assorted warlords were in control. In 1922, they hounded Sun Yat-sen out of Canton and onto a gunboat, where he met a young officer, Chiang Kai-shek. Within three years, Sun was dead and Chiang was left to continue the struggle against the warlords. The real contest was about to begin.

As early as 1918 at Peking University the librarian had set up a society for the study of Marxism. China had always honored intellectuals, and there were communistic elements in native Chinese thought, so the new philosophy was well received.

In 1921, the Chinese Communist party was founded. As long as the new party was weak and the Kuomintang had warlords to fight, the two political groups were able to cooperate. Russia, still consolidating its own revolution, could offer little real support and was divided as to whether to back the Chinese Communists or the Kuomintang. The Kuomintang, at least, seemed to have the strength to break down local feudalism and prepare the ground for the class struggle to come. By the late 1920s, Russia was better able to support revolutions abroad and called for such a response from parties in other countries. In 1927 a small group of Chinese Communists, traditionally oriented toward the urban worker, launched the "Autumn Harvest Uprising." Support was not forthcoming. This Communist group, led by Mao Tse-tung, fled to sanctuary in the country, then to the mountains in southern Kiangsi Province. Recruits came—mutinous soldiers, bandits, and dispossessed peasants. Industrial workers were scarcely represented.

The Long March Meanwhile, Chiang Kai-shek had quelled the warlords. In 1930 he introduced his "bandit-extermination campaign." The "bandits" included the Communists, whom Chiang hoped to starve out of their lairs with a blockade that he set up in 1933. Chiang was nearly successful. At the point of starvation, however, 90,000 Communists and "bandits" broke through the Kuomintang encirclement and started on a flight of some 6,000 miles that led across twelve provinces, through forests and miasmic jungles, and over eighteen mountains. Battles with the Kuomintang were frequent, but some 20,000 Communists went all the way. They escaped not only Chiang's pursuit but also, though they might not have realized it at the time, Russian-dictated communism.

The heroic trek had diminished their numbers. But it had given the survivors fierce loyalty and confidence, together with a charismatic leader, Mao Tse-tung. No city-born worker-oriented, traditional Marxist, Mao came of peasant stock, and he had been reared by a mother who was a devout Buddhist. Throughout the Long March, he had kept bright the new faith, and he had done it without benefit of Communist workers or Russian aid. He had done it with farmers and the dispossessed of the countryside.

The Chinese Communists might still have been overcome,

but for the anticipation of the invasion of China by Japan. Moscow called for a popular front against the Axis. Mao and his diminished band, who were about to be finally gobbled up by the Kuomintang, called on Chiang's pursuing generals to unite with them against the Japanese. Though Chiang doggedly viewed the Communists as his prime enemy, his subordinates regarded internal politics as less of a threat than the foreign foe. They made Chiang a virtual prisoner and forced him to accept the united front against Japan. Tacitly united again, the Kuomintang bore the atrophying brunt of the Japanese attacks. Meanwhile, the Communists shouted patriotic slogans as they recruited and consolidated for the inevitable struggle to come. By the war's end, the Kuomintang was impoverished and depleted, while the Communists rode the crest of the victorious wave. A pretense of mutual goodwill was maintained until 1946, mainly for the sake of United States support. Then the final struggle began. Within two years, mainland China was in Communist hands.

The People's Republic China suffered difficult and severe social problems: corruption in politics, chaos in economics, ignorance, illiteracy, and superstition on a staggering scale. The appeal of the new People's Republic that the Communists had declared was immense. For the long run, of course, a millennium was promised in the Marxist-Leninist form: abolition of class distinction, affluence, the withering away of the state. But unlike the workers' revolt as conceived by Marx and Engels, the task in China fell to the peasants. Initially, with only five million avowed Communists, the existing Chinese government had to be kept functioning. Foreign businesses were at first tolerated, then exploited. The usual procedure was to force the businesses to employ larger and larger labor forces at higher and higher wages. The anticipated result was bankruptcy, with the benefits falling into the workers' hands and the failure vaguely attributable to sabotage on the part of the foreign companies themselves. Even such superficial tolerance of foreign investment vanished with the Korean War in the 1950s. Then the counterrevolutionaries were hunted with the so-called three-anti drive against corruption, waste, and bureaucracy. This drive was followed by a five-anti drive against tax evasion, bribery, theft of state assets, use of knowledge of state economic projects for private gain, and misuse of labor and materials. The ill-famed "mitrailleurs of Lyons" of the French Revolution saw 2,000 executions. In Kwangtung Province alone, by the end of 1951, 28,000 people had been put to death, but Mao was getting results.

Mao Tse-tung For half a billion Chinese, Mao was Marx, Lenin, and Stalin rolled into one. His little red book, *Quotations from Chairman Mao Tse-tung,* guarded and studied like Holy Writ, is actually a simplistic effort to bridge the gap between West and East: between European Marxism and the realities of China. His principle contribution to communism was, of course, the innovation of a rural, guerrilla-type Communist revolution as distinct from that based on worker-oriented urban cells. Lenin had contemplated such possibilities and had made use of his peasants, but it took Mao to demonstrate conclusively that it is in the backward agricultural areas of the world today, not in the highly industrialized, that the Communist appeal is likely to be most effective.

Of more limited importance is Mao's concept of political indoctrination based on the Chinese intellectual tradition of Confucian mind-training. It is this approach that has led to the endless posters and banners, the loudspeaker announcements, the "struggle meetings," and the tortuous process of *cheng-feng yun-tang* (self-criticizing rectification campaigns) —all aspects of the movement that, taken out of context, make Chinese communism appear bizarre and ludicrous to Western eyes.

It was in large part, too, because of Mao that the rift between China and Russia developed. With two such giants, both victorious in their own right, and with a history of mutual distrust, discord was inevitable. But in the early 1950s Mao could still speak "with love" of the Soviet Union. He badly needed aid then.

The actual rift came with the fall of Stalin and the denunciation by Khrushchev of Stalin's cult of personlity. Mao, by implication, was included. He began calling Khrushchev a "psalm-singing buffoon." The Soviet premier, never at a loss for words, described Mao as "a worn-out boot fit only to stand in a corner." Less openly, Khrushchev went on to explain that communes, the basic unit of Chinese communism, didn't work. "We tried them right after the Revolution," he said. By 1960, Russia withdrew her aid from China and as a result became the scapegoat for all Chinese economic woes.

Two years later, Russia continued sending aircraft to India during that country's clash with China. There were disturbances along the Sino-Soviet border, and war between the Communist giants seemed imminent in 1969. Though the Soviets would suffer, China could only be the loser and began casting about for other friends. While Russia had begun endorsing coexistence with the West and the making of allies through aid, instruction, and example, China called this approach revisionism and a betrayal of the people's war. Superficially, at least, Mao clung to the inevitable-war-with-capitalism theory. Thanks to his own military weakness, it was like threatening the local bully with a big brother. But the Soviet Union had no intention of playing that role. Nevertheless, Mao pressed international objectives along subversive and revolutionary lines.

The Great Leap Forward During this unsettled period, Communist China tried her "Great Leap Forward" and nearly broke her political neck. In 1957, Russia seemed to be prevailing in the space race. The United States was sunk in recession. China had to do something toward the apparently imminent Communist world victory, and so it announced the initiation of an economic and social reorganization of sweeping proportions that would move China directly into a genuine Communist society without going through the intermediate socialist stage. Rapid industrialization was the objective of the new program, and it was to be accomplished through an expansion of the commune system. China implied that it was well ahead of Russian communization and it was now about to leap out of sight.

This broad jump was to be largely the task of the peasants. They had already presumably taken a hop and a skip. The hop had come with the redistribution of land between 1950 and 1952. More prosperous peasants had been classified by the Communists as landlords. Most of them, particularly those who rented land, that is, exploited others, were eliminated, and their land was divided among the lesser peasants. There were 300 million of these, and each received about one-third of an acre. This division did little to increase agricultural production. The skip followed naturally, beginning in 1953 with cooperative farming. Resources were pooled, and, though farmers nominally still owned their land, it was in effect worked in common. By 1958, they were ready for the final jump, the ideal, the people's communes. These were to be involuntary units of up to five thousand families, living and working together in collective agricultural projects and small industrial enterprises.

The first commune was opened at Chengtu and called Sputnik. It was much larger than any cooperative, and it incorporated not only agriculture, but industry, education, public health, all social and most domestic functions, which were removed from individual or family control. It also offered no material incentives—and was unwieldy. The peasants were confused and demoralized. The weather turned bad. Dams, too hastily built, collapsed, and as a result of a campaign to eliminate sparrows, the crops were overrun by insect pests. The result was chaos, and the communes began breaking down into smaller village units.

Industry shared with agriculture in the Great Leap and took the same tumble. Initially, the Communists had made no intrusion on private domestic industry. What there was of it was vital to the postwar economy. Then, gradually, private enterprise began to feel the pressure that had eliminated foreign business. From private business to joint private-state management, the economy was nationalized. In general, as with Communist experience everywhere, nationalization of industry showed good results. While before World War I there wasn't a plant for manufacturing bicycles in China, they were now making 12,000-kilowatt steam turbines and jet planes.

The Great Leap, when it came, showed immediate paper success. Statistics may have been inflated, for gradually transportation snarled, materials ran out, products grew shoddy to keep up the quota, and workers were exhausted, thanks to long hours and the food shortages. By 1962, the Great Leap was over in all but name, and Canada and Australia were putting food on Chinese tables.

Mao next set out to improve his people's minds. He was probably worried that the leap had left many with a sense of disillusionment. In any event, he announced a cultural and spiritual revolution. It was not his first campaign for mental uplift. In 1949, he had instituted a program at the college level to reform intellectual thought through social and political re-education and purification. This operation had involved group discussions, confession, and self-criticism—then, finally, sub-mission and, hopefully, a rebirth. Those who did not fully experience the process knew enough to keep their mouths closed. In fact, by 1957, artists and playwrights seemed to Mao well enough reeducated to put an end to censorship. He publicly announced, "Let One Hundred Schools of Thought Contend, and One Hundred Flowers Bloom." Criticism of the regime was instant, vituperative, and upsetting to Chairman Mao. Not flowers, but stinkweeds had blossomed, to his way of thinking, and within the year a new movement, the "Dedica-tion of Hearts Campaign" was under way. This implied that in-tellectuals had better surrender their hearts to the party or shut up.

The Cultural Revolution But the Cultural Revolution initi-ated in 1966 came at a time of more broadly based discontent. The Great Leap had failed. Relations with Russia were bad. They had soured with several previously promising African countries. An iron broom was needed to sweep the stable clean and make a new spiritual start. That broom was the Red Guard, named for the Russian factory workers who in 1905 bled for the revolution. In China, of course, they were not factory workers, but students, from fifteen years of age up to the early twenties. They were only too happy to close down the uni-versities and take off on "Long Marches" to save the revolu-tion. *The Thoughts* of Mao could be found in every knapsack.

To kick matters off, Mao himself was shown swimming down the Yangtze River, nine miles in sixty-five minutes, an Olympic record. With such an example, the Red Guards ran wild. Their goal was to perfect the human personality and purge it of noncommunist and foreign poisons. Up went xenophobic wall posters denouncing all who opposed Mao's thought. An end was put to the sale of luxury goods, perfumes, cosmetics, all that might appeal to degenerate neocapitalists. The names of streets and shops incompatible with Mao's thinking were changed. Revisionists were given dunce caps to wear, and they were made to sit on stools while the "revolutionary masses" taunted them and occasionally trampled them to jelly. Ideally, exploitation was being swept away to leave room for devotion to socialist public interest, but very quickly all control was lost and with it all purpose.

The whole reason for choosing the Red Guards for the mission was their subservience to the party rather than to the army, which Mao distrusted. Now he needed the army to limit the hysteria, which went so far as to invade the sanctity of a Soviet merchant ship in the port of Dairen, humiliate its captain, and provoke a dangerous international incident. There were armed clashes in the streets and untold casualties; there were even rumors of civil war in China. Then, gradually, the turbulence subsided. Schools reopened with some reluctance on the part of staff and students. But by this time the party apparatus was in shambles and the army, while carrying Mao through the crisis, had grown to ominous stature.

The fiasco of the Cultural Revolution must have come as a sobering slap in the face for all concerned. For the radical Red Guards the outcome was more than a mere slap. It meant jail or a firing squad or flight to Hong Kong. Now farmers are more regularly working their own private plots, and, in the provinces, soldiers have replaced the police. What some would call bureaucratic revision and others pragmatic conservatism has moved to the fore in China. That communism, the party, and Mao survived the disaster at all was owed to a generally strong nationalism and the widespread realization that, despite occasional blunders, communism had done much for China. It can be said today that communism has achieved the political unification of a vast and diverse land. It has stamped out banditry, warlordism, and exploitation by foreign powers, as well as much disease and starvation. Under communism, China at last stands up in the modern world and casts a mighty shadow. As has been said, "Once everything changed except China; now, in China, all changes." This is recognized with pride by the average Chinese, who did not go uninformed in 1970 when the government orbited its first small satellite, happily broadcasting the singsong tune: "Dong Fang Hong"—"The East Is Red." Domestically, Mao had done well by the average Chinese citizen, but achieving a plateau of sufficiency from which some other form of government might more usefully lead is still far in the future.

China Today The leadership of the People's Republic of China was shared, until 1976, between the eighty-two-year-old peasant demigod Mao Tse-tung and his sophisticated, worldly mandarin deputy, seventy-six-year-old Chou En-lai, with the weight of responsibility falling more and more to the younger man. Then on January 8, Chou was dead, and Mao was ailing. Contestants for power had for several years been making trouble and now they conspicuously included Mao's wife, Chiang Ch'ing. When Mao finally expired in September the struggle reached its peak. Chiang Ch'ing and her allies—referred to by the more moderate faction as "The Gang of Four" —tried to seize control, failed, and were imprisoned. Then, in a relatively bloodless succession, Hua Kuo-feng became Mao's successor as chairman of the Communist party and Teng Hsiao-ping, the deputy prime minister. The process is symbolically dramatized in Mao's memorial hall. At the entrance stands a dramatic statue of the former leader, the Mao of old. Within, housed in a crystal crypt, are his shrunken remains, suggesting that even gods are mortal. On the wall is a painting of Mao, his hand fondly upon Hua's hand, with the legend, "With you in charge, I can rest."

With the new order installed it is appropriate to look for change in China. The first sign of this was an official statement describing the time of political turmoil as "ten years lost". Indeed, during the years when Mao was failing and Chou En-lai struggled with the radical coalition, industry was neglected. Now the economy is moving ahead slowly. But whereas Mao saw dedication to the Communist ideal as sufficient motivation, today workers' wages are being increased, with bonuses offered for increased factory production. Of course an appeal to the profit motive is to give ground to capitalism, but this second generation of leaders is understandably more pragmatic than its forebearers. Formerly, acceptance into higher education depended primarily upon the purity of the applicant's political attitudes. Now the emphasis has shifted to his performance on written examinations.

While these are policy decisions diverging from the classless ideal of communism, spontaneous practices are developing, sometimes based on influence, sometimes on kinship. This makes for inequality while easing the official program of austerity for a few. To use money for special favors would be to commit criminal bribery. But in China there is an ancient practice called "Kwan Ksi"—signifying good relations between friends. So, out of pure friendship, a man might give piano lessons to a physician's child, and when the piano teacher or a member of his family fell ill, the physician, purely out of friendship, would see that he was placed in one of the few first-class hospitals. A theater manager might bestow free tickets on a butcher, and receive in exchange a supply of otherwise almost unobtainable spareribs. This clearly goes against the ideal of complete equality, for a person with more favors to give is in a position to receive more in return. Then, too, there are the so-called "friendship stores," which originally offered otherwise unavailable foods, clothing, and antiques, but only to foreigners. Now Chinese bureaucrats with special identity cards are shopping there as well. An additional source of outside luxuries for the informed insider are unclaimed gifts sent by Chinese living abroad. Since the intended recipient must pay a duty amounting to the full value of the gift, many go unclaimed, and are subsequently sold to those who can afford them. As yet these practices are not that widespread, particularly outside the urban centers. To the extent they do exist and are spreading they suggest a return to precommunist habits. And they represent an erosion of the classless dreams of Mao and his followers.

There are changes, too, on the international scene. The

Cultural Revolution did much to alter China's relationship with the rest of the world. As long as it raged, China existed in a partial quarantine. Subsequently China returned to the international scene, somewhat chastened. True, Mao's successor, Hua Kuo-feng, seems as unreceptive as his predecessor to overtures from the Soviet Union, and Peking acknowledged the sixtieth anniversary of Russian Communism with an editorial branding the Kremlin leadership as the greatest hazard to world peace. Otherwise, China is courting foreign visitors from East and West. A particular effort has been made in the Afro-Asian area, an effort no longer directly keyed to world revolution. Then there was the celebrated "ping-pong" diplomacy of the early 1970s, culminating in President Nixon's visit to China and the country's acceptance into the United Nations. That first euphoric pace has not been maintained, but there has been no real backing away either. The stumbling block in the way of closer relations between the United States and mainland China remains the island of Taiwan, which the United States has pledged to defend and which the People's Republic would like to absorb.

What does the future have in store for China? With a third of the world's population now living under Marxist governments, and well over half this number Chinese, the question is of global significance. Dogmatic communism in China is undoubtedly not out of gas, but it is clearly suffering engine trouble. This is probably a good thing for the world, though in the long run, if serious trouble comes from China, it is more likely to come from overpopulation than it is from Communist doctrine. China is a giant, the very creature of its own ancient mythology that held that the earth was carved out by a Titan who, at his death, became the elements; his flesh the soil, his blood the rivers and oceans. The race of humans were the parasites feeding on his remains. There is a limit to such a corpse, but seemingly not to the Chinese people. The government has made a major effort at birth control, with factory workers ideally sitting down in groups to decide which couples will restrain themselves so that the baby quotas will not be exceeded. Despite some reported success with such methods, with postponed marriages and sterilization, the fact remains that there are already too many Chinese for their own good. Their numbers, which increase at the rate of 15 million a year, soon will total over a billion. The question is, how long can the stumbling leaps of Mao's followers keep ahead of the alternatives—expand or starve?

The Third World
and Communism

Caught between the dark past and the cybernetic future, between colonialism and independence, between the pressures of capitalism and communism, are many individual nations in large areas of the globe sometimes grouped together and called the Third World. These emergent nations are found in the Arabic Middle East, in black Africa, and in Southeast Asia. Considering these areas together is justified on the basis of certain elemental factors that are common to all of them. All of these areas were formerly largely controlled by white Western capitalism. In the space of half a century, not only has that control been removed, but the invincible image of the white Westerner has been shattered by two world wars and the withdrawals of France and the United States from Indochina. There is now high motivation among the peoples of these areas to make good on their own merits, an objective made difficult by massive poverty, endemic disease, and want of education. Sometimes helping, often hindering, and always confusing these nations in their efforts at self-improvement is the competition between ideologies—capitalism, socialism, and communism—all striving to show the way into the future. Communist assertions have naturally been received diversely by each and every country in this Third World, and, for the sake of an orderly discussion, it must be separated into the areas mentioned above.

The Middle East In the Arabic Middle East, the ancient lands stretching from Morocco to Iraq, a common religious heritage exists. Though the conquests of Islam at one time encompassed a vast empire, there has been much decay, colonizing, and breaking away. Islam, though still a strongly shared experience, is no longer the binding force that it was. Today there are twenty Arab nations: democracies, monarchies, socialist republics, and tyrannies. What does bind together this mass of humanity, with its kings, princes, presidents, and dictators, is a common language: Arabic. More than a language, Arabic closely involves religion and is a way of thinking. This is what one has in mind when one speaks of the Arab mentality and the Arab world. World War II and its consequences ushered in another binding element—the creation of Israel on Arab soil. To the Arabs, Israel's claim to the Holy Land is no more legitimate than was the claim of the Italians when they invaded Libya and put spotlights on the statues of the Caesars. Both are expressions of colonialism under which Egypt and much of the Arab world labored for centuries.

Domestically, communism has had hard going in the area. Its early pre-World War II cells attracted primarily members of the foreign minorities: Jews, Greeks, French. Many of these Communists have been thrown out of the Arab countries, while communism at the Arabic grass roots has been a failure. It is looked upon as a foreign and godless import for which the average Arab has no use and no frame of reference. Sometimes, for the sake of favors from Russia, local parties have been tolerated as long as they undertook no revolutionary activities. Yet from Marrakesh to Baghdad, jails are crowded with Arab Communists.

Typical was the suppression in Sudan, where the Arab world's largest Communist party was broken up in the summer of 1971, and the leaders, including a Lenin Peace Prize winner, were executed. Despite this violence and evidence that Soviet military advisors were involved in the domestic subversion, Russian MIG fighters and tanks are too much of a temptation for Sudan to break off relations with Russia. For Russia, Sudan is an important bridge between the Middle East

COMMUNISM

and black Africa. And so for practical reasons, they too, will undoubtedly swallow their pride.

Egypt The ambivalence shown in Sudan toward communism is typical of the entire Arab world. Included is Egypt, which until Sadat's 1977 mission to Israel was the Arab world's international voice—if the Arabs can be said ever to have had one voice. Egypt has long disavowed communism, and its local adherents, coming mostly from Greek, Jewish, and Armenian minorities, are familiar with Egyptian prison life. Yet under Nasser, Egypt became increasingly dependent on Soviet aid and advisors and domestically evolved a system with communistic overtones.

President Gamal Abdel Nasser christened his new approach "Arab socialism," which for him meant socialism responsive to the particular needs of the Arab community and subject to no imported dogma. The economy and everything governmental was in a shambles in 1952 when Nasser supplanted the playboy King Farouk with his clique of Free Officers. Nasser's evolving system of Arab socialism called for nationalization of the Suez Canal, of banking, and of big industry. There were to be workers' representatives on the board of directors of each company, and each worker was to receive an incentive share of the profits. Retail outlets, artisans, and small enterprises were not controlled. As far as it went, the approach was socialist, the application totalitarian, and the results disappointing.

In the agricultural area, Nasser had grown up with a sincere hatred of the big absentee landowners. They could and did fly in their dinners from Maxim's in Paris while their private armies drove the serfs, the fellahin, out from their fly-infested mud huts to work in the fields. Nasser's love for the oppressed fellahin was personal and sincere, and his measures in their behalf were restrained in the light of such provocations as they suffered. Maximum landholdings were cut to two hundred acres, later to one hundred. There was no intention of collectivizing the villages. In fact, at this lower level, life remained very democratic and unregimented.

Briefly, to contrast Nasser's Arab socialism with communism, it was similar in that its methods at the upper levels were totalitarian and its objectives socialist. In theory, the differences are great. God is acknowledged, and no stateless paradise anticipated. Private ownership at the lower levels, as long as it is not exploitative, is encouraged. Where assets were seized by the state, bonds have been given to former owners in compensation, with a ceiling set on income.

What are Egypt's prospects? They seem uncertain at best. The Aswan Dam, built with Soviet aid, and in which so much hope was placed, is a questionable success. The population is rapidly expanding, and the economy, drained by military expenditures, has been kept afloat by funds from neighboring Arab oil producing nations. The sudden death in 1970 of President Nasser raised many questions. Nasser was an Arab Lincoln, risen up from a modest family in a village of the Beni Mor, "The tribe of the bitter," to his height as "Champion of Arabism, Hero of Socialism." A half million throats would proclaim his name as his open car pressed through seething crowds. His successor, President Anwar el Sadat, seemed at first a mild-mannered man with none of Nasser's natural charisma. But in terms of measurable achievements he soon surpassed his predecessor.

Sadat immediately had Russia to contend with. In the mid-1950s, Egypt needed help. The United States might have given it, but Secretary of State John Foster Dulles' refusal of aid to the Aswan High Dam project, a gap filled by Russia, began a rift that widened irrevocably as the United States increased its military aid to Israel. Egypt wanted counterbalancing armaments and received them from Russia. Along with the aid came memories of colonialism. And it was with conflicting thoughts that President Sadat, in 1971, purged pro-Soviet plotters from his government, while almost at the same time, he entered into a fifteen-year treaty evidently binding Egypt even more closely to the Soviet Union. Yet the tide began to turn. The following year, 20,000 Soviet military personnel were expelled from Egypt. Then in 1973 came the October war with Israel, a triumph for Sadat in that Egypt, though not victorious, was not again humiliated on the field. Of course Egypt's improved fighting ability was largely thanks to Soviet training and arms. It was the subsequent efforts of Secretary of State Henry Kissinger that settled the military stalemate and lifted President Sadat's respect for the United States, at Soviet expense. By 1974 President Nixon had been warmly welcomed in Cairo, and the private sector of the economy, which had narrowed under Nasser, was again being encouraged. By 1976 relations with Russia had soured to the extent that the friendship treaty was broken off and a military cooperation agreement signed with China. Matters came to a crisis in the winter of 1977 when Sadat surprised the world by announcing his resolve to achieve a peace settlement with Israel. A number of Arab nations, Syria, Libya, Iraq, South Yemen, and Algeria, those which still court Soviet arms if not Soviet politics, ranked themselves in opposition. Saying that Russia only wanted to keep the area in turmoil so that their weapons and advisors would be needed, Sadat emphasized this verbal slap by closing all Soviet cultural offices, as well as those run by Russia's Communist allies: Czechoslovakia, East Germany, and Poland. Just what will come of Sadat's bold diplomacy remains to be seen. He has certainly risked a great deal in what is a very courageous gamble, and for the moment, at least, Communist influence in Egypt has reached a low ebb.

To sum up briefly—domestic communism has very poor prospects throughout the Arab world. As former President Abdul Salam Aref of Iraq declared, "Islam alone is absolute justice. We do not need to import principles from abroad." The ruling family of Saudi Arabia, in addition to safeguarding their own rule and the Saudi oil industry, is intent equally in furthering Islam and combating communism, radicalism, and Zionism. Putting power struggles, which are constant, aside, the general drift is toward Arab socialism along totalitarian and military lines. The chief goal is land reform. This does not imply, as in Russia, the replacement of one class by another, or communization, but ideally a cooperation between private and public sectors with no one being exploited.

Internationally, the emphatic goal of most Arab nations is self-determination. Nonalignment is a cornerstone of policy. Some have called it "positive neutrality," which implies a willingness to accept aid, without commitment, from East or West. Soviet Russia has been favored in recent years as a direct result of Arab antagonism toward Western-supported Israel. Traditional anti-Semitism in Russia has encouraged this support, particularly of the Palestine Liberation Organization, which through its terrorist activities has repeatedly impeded efforts toward a peaceful Mideastern settlement. Ironically the Arabs share little of this fundamental prejudice and religiously acknowledge a common heritage with the Jews. What scalds and what has often turned Arab countries toward Russia is the conviction that Israel is the last thorny creature of an old and loathed tradition of Western imperialism. This specter, which has haunted the Arab world since Queen Victoria's day, suggests similar Soviet aspirations toward the Middle East. The threat now seems too great to make Russian aid appealing as long as hopes for a diplomatic settlement remain high.

Black Africa   To the south, beyond the deserts of North Africa, are numerous emergent nations, some small, all militantly separate, but united in terms of the experience of color. This is black Africa, and in its sometimes strident, boisterous youth, it has been tempted by a variety of ideologies, not the least influential of which is communism.

Quite apart from outside pressures, there are local factors that enhance communism's appeal in the area. For the black intelligentsia who face a confused future, the system offers clear-cut techniques for manipulating society toward a more industrial and, presumably, a more successful future. Then, too, it seems to have an inherent kinship with the natural communism of the traditional tribes, where herds and the fruits of the hunt were held in common. In a historical perspective, communism repudiates the centuries of exploitation by white men that are the African's cruel memory: the slave trade that led to the captivity and death of tens of millions of black Africans and more recently the Western competition for the natural resources of the continent.

Factors detrimental to the flowering of communism in black Africa, however, seem to have greater weight. There is the "blackness" of Africa, to begin with. Going beyond the physical reality, it carries a spiritual significance that cannot be shared beyond that continent. It is the basis for the Pan-African movement and for much nationalistic sentiment. It binds Africans together just as the Arabs are bound by a common religion and language. Tribalism, though it has communistic tendencies, also has democratic ones, such as the practice of giving every man a vote. An inherent tendency to acquiesce to the authority of important chiefs encourages despotism when tribal ways yield to modern statehood. Loyalties shift slowly, from tribe to nation, but already in the more urban areas where leadership first develops, tribalism has largely given way to nationalism.

Colonialism, like tribalism, is a two-edged sword. While the memory of it may leave hostility to Western ideas and control, it does not automatically make communism attractive. For, though Russia and China may protest to the contrary, both have been guilty of imperialism. Like her Arab neighbors to the north, black Africa wants economic help but no more administration from abroad. Though Hungary and Tibet are more distant than tribal memories of the slave trade, the implications for modern Africa are not discounted. Finally, like the Arabs, black Africans have a strong religious background. Christianity and Islam are less deeply ingrained than their own animism of invisible forces and beings and the spirit world of their ancestors, but all are incompatible with Communist materialism. At a more superficial level, when it comes simply to selecting a convenient trading partner, the democratic West (and economically and politically this includes Japan) has more to offer in terms of development and advanced business techniques.

Though the dice may be loaded against them there, neither Russia nor China can be accused of not trying to influence Africa. Until recently, these Communist countries had seemed more remote than the moon to the average African. But starting from zero, in the mid-1950s, thousands of Soviet and Chinese technicians began to arrive in Africa, while hundreds of African students were invited to Moscow University. This approach certainly did not reflect the thinking of Karl Marx, who had concentrated his future hopes on the industrial society. Africa was beyond his ken; a blank on the map. Lenin was the Communist theorist who first realized the potential of underdeveloped colonial countries. He had rationalized for them a drift from precapitalism straight to communism without the Marxist requisite of a capitalistic period. This prediction was gratifying to all enthusiastic Communists after their early failures in industrial Europe. Nevertheless, during the formative 1920s, Lenin concluded that the proletariat in the colonial countries was too weak to bother with, and his approach would be to support bourgeois democratic forces as a way of gaining influence. It sounded like a practical idea. In operation, however, antifascism became a necessary preoccupation until after 1948, which left Soviet communism little time for African affairs.

Once Communist power in Eastern Europe had been consolidated, however, the Soviets again looked to Africa. In Stalin's view, the world was divided into two irreconcilable camps, the imperialist and the anti-imperialist blocs. He included Russia in the latter despite recent Soviet activity in Eastern Europe and the Balkans. Applying Marxist-Leninist dogma to the colonies in Africa, Stalin decided there would be an inevitable revolt brought on by increasing imperialist oppression from the West. With this in mind, it was the Communist task to prepare the revolutionaries, and the Soviets already had training centers such as the "University of the Eastern Toilers" at Tashkent in the USSR.

The Soviet Union readied itself for a long struggle, only to be taken by surprise. With very little hesitation, most of the Western colonial powers granted the black African states their independence. This ideological disaster for the Communists occurred about the same time as Stalin's denunciation by Khrushchev. Doggedly Moscow began rethinking her policies in the light of the new black African spirit. The national bourgeoisie of these African countries was rehabilitated into a worthy ally, and Russian goals were altered to a long-term political speculation. The hope was to break down fears of the Soviet Union and at the same time gain influence by force of example. Houses of Soviet culture were set up. Black students were invited to the Soviet Union for free education and indoctrination. For those who could not go, film vans went out to the villages. They showed how much the Soviet Union loved black people, as well as what work huge Russian-made tractors were capable of doing. In this way, subversion and governmental overthrow gave way to a policy of winning allies in the cold war. The old monolithic goal of one look-alike Communist world was replaced by a more practical one of competing with the old Western imperialists for spheres of influence through the use of economic aid and trade.

China's approach to the black African scene has been different. Though unable to afford the massive aid doled out by Soviet Russia, it has two advantages. First, her people are not white, a racial factor that has its value, although it is theoretically of no importance in Marxist thinking. Secondly, modern Russia in many ways resembles the former European colonial powers. It is industrialized, while China is still in the process. Africans see things going on in agricultural China that they can immediately apply to their own country.

These similarities and differences in background do not, however, account for the difference in the Chinese and Soviet approaches to Africa, which until fairly recently has been a factor in Sino-Soviet discord. In the Peking view, to support bourgeois Africa, as Russia was doing, was to work against the revolution, a feeling going back to their own experience with Chiang Kai-shek. Consequently, Chinese aid was initially limited to nations susceptible to revolution. Others, including Nasser's Egypt, were denounced and written off as imperialist puppets. China's Premier Chou En-lai toured ten promising African countries in the winter of 1963–64, and subsequently Radio Peking bombarded them with anti-American, anticolonial messages. Ironically, the speeches were delivered in English. Only recently has the Peking hard line begun to thaw. The trend today seems to be toward promoting allies rather than stirring up revolution.

Given the black African setting and the Communist approach, what results have been achieved? A flavor of the changing scene can be given by briefly considering examples of former Belgian, French, Portuguese and British colonies, their different preparations for independence, and their reaction to Communist infiltration.

Zaïre Nowhere was preparation for independence more inadequate than in the Belgian Congo. The Belgian policy provided very limited educational facilities in the Congo but absolutely no political training for the Congolese in how to run an independent country. As late as 1956, Belgium was blandly discussing the possibility of independence within thirty years. Within two years there was rioting in the Congo, within four, a panicked Belgium was pulling out, leaving the huge, tribalized country adrift in the twentieth century, with no established political leaders and exactly twenty-four college graduates. There were numerous aspirants to leadership. Among them was a former postal employee and convicted embezzler, Patrice Lumumba, who escalated the growing confusion first by calling on the United Nations to give aid in what was clearly a tribal dispute and very soon thereafter calling for Russian troops.

The Russians were all too ready to apply their simple class-struggle theories to the complicated crosscurrents of tribalism, nationalism, and personal egoism. The tumult increased until General Joseph Mobutu, the head of the army, took over. The Russians were told to depart and they did, leaving the Congo to a more hopeful future. Lumumba was handed over to Katanga tribesmen, who amused themselves by taking him apart slowly: an ear, a nose, a toe, one by one.

President Mobutu Sese Seko has evaded intrigues of rival leaders and dissident tribes. His prospects are enhanced by a potentially rich economy, and though the Republic of Zaïre, the former Congo, is subject to increasingly repressive measures, it has growing stability. The nationalization of foreign-owned agricultural lands and mines might be seen as communistic, but in fact was the most practical method of eliminating foreign influence in Zaïre. In 1975 the United States fell from grace with President Mobutu when the CIA was accused of plotting his assassination. But within the year U.S. military help was being sought for Mobutu's brother-in-law, Holden Roberto, whose supporters in neighboring Angola were losing out to a Soviet-backed takeover there. For the forseeable future Zaïre will go its own way, accepting help when it is offered but being very cautious about the strings which always seem to be attached to international gifts.

Guinea Unlike the paternal Belgian approach, the French wanted to remake their colonials, by their own choice or not, into French citizens. Whenever possible, this meant a French education and some slight introduction to the governmental process. As in the Congo, independence came abruptly to French Guinea in 1958, when Charles de Gaulle put forth a referendum offering French overseas territories their choice of integration with France or complete independence.

Unlike the Congo, Guinea already had a popular hero in Sékou Touré, a member of the old clan known as the "Sword Nobility." His answer to French President de Gaulle was, "We prefer poverty in liberty to riches in slavery." De Gaulle gave his civil servants sixty days to clear out. "Too slow," thundered Touré, and within eight days the French were gone. But for Touré, chaos would have reigned. He took over in an underdeveloped land of diverse tribal loyalties. His own political theories were neither democratic nor entirely communist. "Communism is not the way for Africa," he said, though he adopted certain Marxist forms. For class warfare, he substituted anticolonial struggle, and he used the heretic cult of the individual as successfully as Hitler or Mao.

Soviet communism approached this relatively settled state with far more caution than it was to show in invading the Congo. Not arms but a tactful ambassador, Daniel Solod, arrived, and after him came a horde of advisors and technicians. Though the farmers seemed to resent the new collective approach, Russia soon began speaking confidently of the new "people's democracy." As soon as Guinea appeared to have burnt its bridges to the West, however, aid began to dry up. Domestic crises were encouraged to hasten Guinea into the Soviet camp. When promised food arrived from the USSR it was spoiled. Grain was already fermenting. Instead of vital tractors came snowplows and toilet seats. Sugar was so treated for humidity that it refused to dissolve in tea.

Despite these problems, the Soviets felt that their plan was working. Procommunist Guineans paraded and rioted in the streets. Once again, however, Russia had jumped the gun. Touré wasn't about to be overturned by a Russian-inspired conspiracy. In December, 1961, he threw out Ambassador Solod. His objective was not a complete shift to the West, but he knew that Russia was aware that the West would only too happily step in. He was not overly surprised when Anastas Mikoyan hurried to Guinea to smooth things over.

As of 1974 Guinea called itself a one-party republic and Sékou Touré was unopposed in initiating his third seven-year presidential term as dictator, with a police state to support him. A less self-assured Soviet Union has seen to it that Guinea's small army was equipped with Russian helmets and Czech rifles. Refusing to be won over, Touré sacrilegiously described communism as nothing but state capitalism. By 1976, after eighteen years, relations with France had warmed to the extent that ambassadors were exchanged and the following year Guinea sent a delegation to Washington, exploring prospects of improved relations, a gesture made more emphatic by the ending of Soviet reconnaissance flights from Guinea. First and foremost, Touré is loyal to himself and then to Africa. What happens next is an open question. The vacuum that will exist after Touré will have to be filled, and it is unlikely to be a smooth process.

Ghana Of all the colonial powers in Africa, only Britain acted as though the subjects might eventually become independent. She took the responsibility of training them in self-government. Until 1957, the British Gold Coast basked in the old dream of a bygone kingdom of Ghana ruled over by kings so rich they tethered their horses to gold nuggets. Then part of the dream came true. As the first liberated colony in black Africa, Ghana was reborn, and with this rebirth came a ruler nearly as fabulous as the monarchs of old. This was Kwame Nkrumah, Ghana's first president. He was born in a mud hut and his name means "Saturday's child." Nkrumah studied at Lincoln University in Pennsylvania and was impressed early on by the American Marcus Garvey and his back-to-Africa movement.

Influenced by African tradition, Western education, and the lure of Marxism, Nkrumah described himself as a "Christian, Marxist, socialist." As president he tended to mix up Marxian theory with the Bible, and for good measure he tied to the arms of his chair of state leather voodoo charms to repel evil spirits. Postcards from Ghana pictured Jesus and Nkrumah hand in hand. In practice Nkrumah ruled less by messianic love than by fascist police power. Nkrumah's one mistake as a dictator was not to destroy the opposition of tribal chiefs as Touré did in Guinea. A hard core of resistance existed in the Ashanti tribe, and in 1966, while Nkrumah was on his way to visit Peking, the Ashantis rose along with the army, abolished his party, and told him never to return.

Under an army-led National Liberation Council, Lieutenant General Joseph Ankrah took over the government. Ankrah favored friendship with Britain. The British had not been ousted from Ghana in anger as had been the French from Guinea and the Belgians from the Congo. However, faced with accepting Ghanian citizenship or getting out of the country, an alternative colored by Nkrumah's constant harping on the evils of colonialism, many British subjects departed. Still, much private capital remained in the hands of Western businessmen and leading Ghanians retained a taste for things British: the judges' robes, afternoon tea, cricket on the green, a culture and philosophy were retained in form if not entirely in substance. These residual tendencies have been encouraged along with closer Western ties. Under the succeeding prime minister, Kofi A. Busia, the trend seemed toward civilian government, British-style socialism, and a balancing of the economy, which Nkrumah had left several hundred million dollars in the red.

All this was repudiated in January 1972, when the prime minister was ousted and his cabinet ministers jailed, following a military coup led by Colonel Ignatious K. Acheampong. As chairman of the National Redemption Council, Acheampong repudiated Ghana's enormous foreign debt. By lowering certain taxes he has made himself popular in a land that, like so many emergent nations, seems unprepared to cope with democratic government. There is every indication that the Supreme Military Council, headed by Acheampong, who in 1976 elevated himself to general, will stay on indefinitely.

Angola Until 1975 this black African country had been governed by a strictly paternal Portuguese administration. Despite fourteen years of guerrilla warfare, Portugal remained reluctant to shed this last jewel of empire until a political shake-up at home led abruptly in 1975 to a brief transitional government and the decision to yield full independence on November 11. In no way were the people of Angola prepared to take over the running of their country. Three groups, following tribal loyalties and born of the guerrilla war, vied to fill the political gap. The oldest was MPLA, the Popular Movement for the Liberation of Angola. Its leader was and still is Agostinho Neto, the son of a Methodist pastor, who himself has renounced religion for Marxism. MPLA's two rivals, which banded together in the ensuing power struggle, are the FNLA, the National Front for the Liberation of Angola, and UNITA, The National Union for the Total Independence of Angola. The latter combination received trickles of aid from Zaïre and a few white mercenaries from South Africa. It might have received massive aid from the United States as well had not Vietnam remained a bad taste in the mouth of the American public. Sensing this reluctance, the Soviet Union, particularly through its protégé, Cuba, sent in tanks, jets, and infantry. Rival republics were set up but MPLA quickly gained the upper hand and was recognized by most other African nations.

The war goes on, with MPLA and Agostinho Neto controlling the towns with their Cuban troops. Without the Cubans, the regime would probably fall, yet in the long term this alien presence, scarcely less offensive than that of the South African whites, may increase resentment and lend support to MPLA's rivals, who continue to conduct a back-country guerrilla war with growing local support. Meanwhile, Neto presses an economic policy of nationalization and confiscation in both agriculture and industry to increase state ownership and to break down the former Portuguese economic framework. Neto regards his party as "a vanguard of the proletariat with the goal of uniting Marxist workers, peasants and intellectuals to create an orthodox, one party Marxist-Leninist regime." How long it will last in an explosive situation is the question.

Ethiopia and Somalia The 1977–78 dispute between Ethiopia and Somalia, the first African nation to sign a friendship pact with the Soviet Union, is a good example of the mercurial loyalties of black Africa's newly formed "socialist" states. The Republic of Somalia was created on July 1, 1960, when a United Nations trust territory, formerly an Italian colony, was combined with the British protectorate of Somaliland. In 1969 the republic was finished off with the assassination of President Abdulrashid Ali Shermarke. Characteristically, a military council took over, and its revolutionary council immediately sought aid from Russia. Somalia seemed a Communist disciple in the making, with the potential of furnishing the Soviets with strategic naval facilities at Berbera on the Indian Ocean.

But from the beginning the Somali Revolutionary Socialist party had trouble adjusting to the Soviet model. Collectivization comes hard to a country where the majority of the population are livestock raisers, and despite President Mohammed Siyad Barre's insistence that Marx and Islam are compatible, the Koran very flatly encourages private property. When a religious leader was shot for preaching that the Koran denied the equality of the sexes and two Soviet MIGs collided shortly thereafter, the accident was widely accepted by the people as a sign of Allah's anger.

Regardless of widespread popular dissatisfaction with Communist doctrine, the government remained doggedly loyal to the Soviets until 1977, when during a border dispute with Ethiopia, Russia gave support to the latter. In November 1977, Somalia repudiated the friendship pact and all Soviet and Cuban advisors were sent packing, in the obvious hope that the United States would intervene should Ethiopia try to invade Somalia. Another Islamic country, Saudi Arabia, across the Red Sea from the horn of Africa on which Somalia and Ethiopia lie, backed Somalia to counter Soviet support of

Ethiopia. Aided additionally by Cuban mercenaries, Somalian troops were driven from Ethiopian territory in the spring of 1978.

Ethiopia had a long tradition of friendship with the United States under its last feudal ruler, Emperor Haile Selassie. Then in 1974 dissatisfaction with Selassie's government's archaic rule led first to strikes by discontented workers, which the army supported. The aging emperor was put aside, and a military council took his place. The first chairman, Lieutenant General Aman Michael Andom, a moderate, was presently murdered and the more radical Brigadier General Teferi Benti took over, followed in his turn by Lieutenant Colonel Mengistu Haile Mariam, whose objective was to turn Ethiopia into a one-party socialist state. Under the slogan "Ethiopia First," the government seized all property considered useful for economic progress. Press censorship was established, civil rights abrogated, and troublemakers shot. By 1975 reforms were spreading to the countryside, with some 22,000 small peasant associations being established.

With United States' aid cut off from this professedly Marxist regime, Russia was quick to fill the gap. By 1976 American military bases were entirely closed and the dispute with Somalia over the Ogaden region was brewing. By 1977 Russia and Cuba were in the impossible situation of aiding both sides, hypocrisy which Somalia was the first to repudiate.

Just where Ethiopia is headed is uncertain. The prospects are several and none of them very attractive. The military regime still professes a position of nonalignment, but more and more relies upon outside Communist aid to hold off the Somalis, not to mention Eritrean nationalists from the north. Law and order scarcely exist, even in the capital city of Addis Ababa, where people are regularly found shot with notes pinned to their bodies denouncing them as counterrevolutionaries. In fact, Addis Ababa is in a veritable state of internal seige, with government forces battling antimilitary terrorists who also call themselves Marxist. Meanwhile, there are the Soviet and Cuban troops that show little inclination to depart. Ethiopia is, after all, strategically situated in the horn of Africa and Russia would very much like to set up air bases there permanently.

Just how many chapters in the book of communism's adventures in Africa remain to be written is beyond guessing. Among many Cubans the thought of their sons dying in an African war is as repellent as the Vietnam war became in the United States. There remains a very real possibility that Soviet support for the black guerrilla movement in Rhodesia will be beefed up with Cuban troops. Then what? Perhaps the situation in Somalia and Ethiopia suggests something about the outline that will be followed. Aid will be accepted as long as it has few strings, and intervention as well, when it seems crucial to the survival of the regime. But even where communism is experimented with internally, it is a very national business and black Africans are jealous of their new independence and wary of any new version of colonialism, whether it comes from white capitalism or white or yellow communism.

Southeast Asia Southeast Asia lacks the unifying consciousness of blackness found in Africa as well as the pervasive lingual and religious ties that bind the Arab world. With the exception of Thailand, Southeast Asia shares with those other areas only the colonial past and the too-rapid emergence into an ideologically laden future. Along this line, two simplifications exist. One has been endorsed by the United States' policy to the effect that there are in Southeast Asia a number of democracy-loving states that, if unprotected, will fall to international communism like a row of dominoes. The other idea derives from Moscow and Peking and pictures an Asiatic people oppressed by the white West, yearning only to bask in the light of the Communist dawn. Existing simultaneously, these notions make for the more or less constant rattle of machine guns.

Despite the lack of homogeneity, a few generalities for political and ideological purposes can be made about Southeast Asia. First, there is the diversity itself. While the anthropologist struggles with ethnic origins, the average Southeast Asian villager is content with the myth that says the human race comes from seeds strewn from a great pumpkin. Skin tones relate to whether a people's seeds emerged from a hole opened with a knife or from one burned through by a red-hot poker. In addition to ethnic dissimilarities, religions are various: Buddhist, Hindu, Islamic, Christian, animist, with many blends and variations. Languages are almost beyond count. There is very little shared history such as one finds in America, and no shared attitudes such as the African "negritude" as described by Léopold Senghor of Senegal. In short, the peoples of Southeast Asia would seem to lack the uniformity of dominoes for Western fears or Communist purposes.

By and large, the average Southeast Asian is nonpolitical. If a farmer is asked where his people originated, he will answer, "Here, in this village." Here his grandparents lived, and that is horizon enough. This average peasant is conservative and loyal to his landlord, king, or tribal chief. Nationalism and dedication to political causes are recent Western innovations.

In Southeast Asia, apart from a Western-educated and Western-fattened veneer of politicians and professional people, there is no reason for the average citizen to love or respect the white West. Until World War I, the white colonial seemed invincible and superior. That war reduced his prestige, as did the repercussions of the economic depression that followed. Any lingering respect vanished with the Japanese invasion early in World War II. Then the white colonial was humbled, and there was Japanese talk of Asia for the Asians. This boiled down to a Japanese colonial empire, and, with the war going badly for the Japanese, they proved far harsher masters than the ousted Europeans. They left a bad taste behind them, one that China, as a big, threatening, militant neighbor to the north, has done little to dissipate. China's overrunning of Tibet and its attacks along the Indian border have not helped to distinguish it from Japan. Not that the Asians want the Europeans back, either. What most Southeast Asians long for is simply to be left alone.

That's the last wish the Asians are apt to have fulfilled. If they are lucky, they will have political pressure and massive aid programs, as in the case of India. If they are unlucky, they will have all this plus war, subject to foreign manipulation.

Such was the situation in Korea and Vietnam, and to a lesser extent in neighboring Laos and Cambodia.

Vietnam   Vietnam, formerly part of French Indochina, has been a battleground for over thirty years. Communism has been a major factor in the struggle from the first, when a native son returned from the Marxist community in Paris and began to burn tax rolls while robbing and killing French officials. This was Ho Chi Minh. The French ruthlessly crushed his insurrections, a process that only heightened among Ho's people his image as a gallant Robin Hood. During the years of Japanese occupation, Ho built up a guerrilla army, only to find, with the peace, that he was trapped between the menace of Communist China in the north and the demands of the French at home. Fearing the Chinese more, the Vietnamese allowed the French to remain, subject to future negotiations.

A flood of returning French settlers and troops indicated their adamant intention to stay on forever, and Ho renewed the battle against France and the puppet government under Bao Dai. Ho's fighting doctrine for his Communists was, "You are fish in the water, and the water is the people." The French were outmaneuvered and by 1954 were ready to throw in the sponge. By this time, Ho Chi Minh controlled northern Vietnam and the anticommunist Ngo Dinh Diem held the south, with aid from the United States. Diem lasted nine years. In 1963, an assassin finished him, and the long war accelerated again. In the early 1970s the United States began to withdraw its support, leaving an international commission to enforce a cease-fire. They did nothing, and the North Vietnamese overran the demoralized South. On April 30, 1975, Saigon, capital of South Vietnam, surrendered after thirty years of fighting. Considering the old enmities, no blood bath ensued. Banks and industries were nationalized and refugees were encouraged to return to their farms, though many thousands fled abroad. No specific plans for collectivization were made. On July 2, 1976, formal reunification of the two Vietnams was declared, with Hanoi, in the north, the capital, and Saigon renamed Ho Chi Minh City. By November of 1977, bolstered by Russian aid (China remains a traditional foe), Vietnam declared itself open for tourism, while at the same time repudiating the domino theory by escalating its border war with neighboring Communist Cambodia. Officially, these troubles are referred to as minor incidents that can sensibly be solved by Communist brothers. The fact remains that war planes and artillery are involved and casualties have been heavy. Having occupied 400 square miles (1,040 sq km) of Cambodian territory, Vietnam demanded frontier negotiations. Cambodia refused until the Vietnamese forces were withdrawn and on January 31, 1977, broke off diplomatic relations. Hardly the stuff for cementing world communism, there is more at stake here than a quarrel between two small countries over a patch of jungle. China supports the smaller Cambodia and views its invasion by Vietnam as the effort of Soviet revisionism to expand in Southeast Asia. Unless the dispute is contained, China is not likely to passively permit a threat to Cambodian sovereignty.

Laos   Until a few years ago, Laos remained happily isolated from world politics, disturbed only by the feudal power skirmishes of minor princes who spent most of their time banqueting and riding elephants. The people were carefree, isolated, and illiterate, and they were not particularly resentful of their French administrators. Then, abruptly, the French pulled out, leaving a natural vacuum for China, the Soviet Union, North Vietnam, or the United States to fill and exploit. In June 1974, the United States withdrew its forces. Some North Vietnamese troops remained, and a coalition government was proposed, represented by Prince Souvanna Phouma and, for the left, or Pathet Lao, by Prince Souphanouvong. By June of 1975, the U.S. aid program came to an end, and before the year was out the 600-year-old monarchy was abolished, with Prince Souphanouvong taking over as president. Though professedly Communist, the new president maintains that he desires to have good relations with all nations, including the United States.

Cambodia   Cambodia was never a country with Communist leanings. The threat always came from the political whirlpools of neighboring Laos, Vietnam, and Thailand. By 1970 the wars in Vietnam and Laos simply overflowed. The rightist military clique in Cambodia felt obliged to take over from the formerly neutralist Prince Sihanouk, who fled to Peking. With aid from the United States, the new premier, General Lon Nol, resisted encroachment by the Khmer Rouge rebels for a while, then in 1974 tried unsuccessfully to negotiate with them and, seeing the handwriting on the wall, left the capital city of Phnom Penh, taking one million dollars into Hawaiian retirement. Within three weeks, on April 17, 1975, the war ended. It seemed at first a happy relief from years of strife. Prince Sihanouk returned in triumph to be named president for life, but the real power was Khieu Samphan, who had led the guerrilla war. On January 5, 1976, the country was renamed Democratic Kampuchea. Three months later Sihanouk was ousted and Samphan was named the new head of state. By this time the honeymoon was long over. Samphan's black-uniformed army, reminiscent of the Nazi SS, had purged the country of opposition. Thousands were executed. The citizens of Phnom Penh had been forcibly evacuated to the countryside where all over six years of age were forced to work. There are virtually no schools. The soldiers are the one embodiment of authority, replacing Buddhist monks, teachers, and parents. Today Cambodia is a land of poverty without industry or medical or cultural facilities. If indeed the military masters are Communist, their only doctrine is to make the people work, without any ideological speeches about capitalism or communism. Unlike Vietnam, China is favored over the Soviet Union, for while the Soviets kept up relations with Lon Nol until the end, China aided the insurgents. If Cambodia can be said to be an example of the domino theory, its fall certainly did not leave it with world communism but rather a dreary form of military tyranny which made this once colorful little country one of the saddest places on earth.

Korea From 1910 to 1945 the Korean peninsula was under Japanese dominion. Before the end of World War II, Russia and the United States agreed that it would be divided on the 38th parallel into North and South zones of responsibility for effecting the surrender of the Japanese. Once the fighting was over, however, the cold war set in and Russia refused to co-operate in reunifying the country. In 1947 the United Nations sponsored elections in the South alone, and the following year the Republic of Korea was proclaimed in the South. Meanwhile, Russia sponsored the local Communists in the North. Former Japanese assets were nationalized and a Communist government established.

With occupation troops pulled out, both North and South began to re-arm, and on June 25, 1950, the North Koreans advanced, without warning, over the border. To prevent an imminent rout, the United States pressured a reluctant United Nations into countering with a "police action." Dominated by United States' forces, the tide was quickly turned. Unfortunately this counterattack was not content to break off at the 38th parallel but rolled on into the North until Communist China felt entitled to enter the fray with endless waves of human gun fodder. After vast slaughter, the front finally stabilized where it had all begun, at the 38th parallel. An armistice was achieved in 1953.

Throughout the 1950s and 1960s North Korea, under Premier Kim Il-Sung, seemed always on the brink of provoking renewed hostilities. While some economic progress was made, the premier waxed and waned in his loyalties, first identifying ideologically with China, then with the Soviets, and finally, in 1966, declaring North Korea independent of them both. Meanwhile, the expected outburst never materialized and by the end of 1977, under a new prime minister, Li Jong-ok, the former chairman of the heavy industry commission, North Korea had set economic progress as her primary goal and the threat of more bloodletting had subsided.

Indonesia   The Islands of Indonesia were until 1949 part of the Dutch colonial empire. Communism arrived as a party in 1920, prematurely attempted a revolution in 1927, and was easily put down. When Holland finally agreed to recognize an independent Indonesian Republic after World War II, little had been done to prepare the new nation for independence and the government was managed almost single handedly by President Sukarno, who scorned Western parliamentary practice as "chatterbox democracy" and referred to his system as "guided democracy," which in application meant dictatorship. By the mid-1950s he was being wooed by both the Soviet Union and Red China, visited both, received an honorary doctorate from Moscow University, the Order of Lenin, and 100 million dollars in economic aid. His sympathies encouraged the growth of a Communist party in Indonesia. By 1965 its membership had grown to about 3 million. In September of that year with Sukarno's tacit support it made an attempt at seizing control. The army counterattacked, destroyed the party, and killed some 350,000 of its members. With President Sukarno first stripped of power and then ousted, his military replacement, General Suharto, banned the Communist party along with Sukarno's "revolutionary romanticism" and set about the difficult business of repairing an economy wrecked by neglect and reckless spending. Despite an almost comical coup attempted by a Javanese mystic in 1976, Suharto remains popular and as anticommunist as ever.

India Southern Asia's largest nation and one in which Communist infiltration has fortunately taken a milder form than elsewhere is India. Lenin expected communism to succeed in India—overcrowded, poor beyond belief—before it did in China. History has frustrated his hopes and hopelessly divided the Communist party in India. The main cause of communism's defeat was the political and religious leader Mahatma Gandhi, who united much of India behind him in his nonviolent drive for independence. Not only was he successful in ousting the British after World War II, he made great strides in dispelling the sense of class and the potential class warfare that is such a primary Communist instrument.

The Communist party of India (CPI) got off to a promising start in the early 1920s, quite oblivious of the endless frustrations to come. Their first mistake, made under Soviet direction, was to oppose Gandhi's movement as bourgeois deception. This position immediately estranged the party from the mainstream of progress. The end of World War II brought the British withdrawal, the success of Gandhi's cause, and his assassination. Left to govern the country was the Congress party, run by Westernized, university-educated Indians. The Communists tried hard to adapt, going so far in the state of Tripana as to campaign for the restoration of a former maharajah—anything to gain popularity.

Real problems for the CPI began with the Sino-Soviet rift. Traditionally the party had Soviet roots, but socially India was better fitted for the Chinese approach. There existed in India no substantial industrial bourgeoisie to be overthrown. While one group in the CPI held to the Russian-sanctioned policy of seeking political victory by parliamentary means and accepted a general reconciliation with Nehru's socialist policies, the more militant faction advocated overthrow of the government by guerrilla tactics. This "Chinese" minority received a near deathblow in 1962, when China attacked along the Indian frontier. The CPI offices in New Delhi were sacked, and the party rightists called for unity in defense of the Indian motherland. China accused the Indian Communists of national chauvinism, and the pro-Chinese leftist branch of the party set up a parallel party organization, which in 1964 held a separate party congress in Calcutta, while the Russian-oriented majority met in Bombay. The CPI has recovered from the low ebb of those days, but the average Indian still feels no affection for the Chinese behemoth to the north or for the puppet party that carries out its policies in India.

If the local Communist party has proved weak and the Chinese a menace, relations with the Soviet Union have been very close until the recent fall of Prime Minister Indira Gandhi, no relation to Mahatma Gandhi. In 1971 a friendship treaty was signed with Russia, and under her administration, India moved toward dictatorship with the arrest of political opposition, the suppression of dissent, and individual rights subordinated to the government's definition of the national interest. Then in March 1977, Mrs. Gandhi's "emergency" regime was voted out of office. The following year Mrs. Gandhi had entirely severed her relations with the old Congress party and had established a fragmented following under the slogan "Forward to Socialism." The road back will be a long one for Mrs. Gandhi, and meanwhile the Soviet Union has lost its most important ally in Asia. Her successor is 82-year-old Morarji Desai, who has freed political prisoners, put an end to censorship, and promised a return to a policy of "proper nonalignment," which existed before Mrs. Gandhi. Desai, an ardent anticommunist, favors small private business concerns to big national ones. It is, of course, understandable for these private businesses to look toward the West and its more lucrative markets than toward the Soviet Union or China. Nevertheless, with a fast growing and generally impoverished population of over 600 million, India's basic problems remain. For the present, at least, they are contained within a democratic context.

The Future   More than any other large area of the world, Southeast Asia as well as India lack the common thread that would provide for a facile summing up. About all that can be said by way of generalization is that a large, uneducated, agrarian mass of diverse humanity has been thrust by recent colonialism into political and ideological turmoil. All of the people are impressed by the power of the United States and China, and they are afraid of both. For many, Russia, though equally awesome, may seem a happy compromise, for it has been the Soviet policy there to give aid without strings in hope of wooing the national governments, while the United States and China pull right and left.

It has been the mistake of the United States to see only ill-fitting extremes, Western democracy or Eastern communism, while disregarding thousands of years of religious, racial, and ethnic accord and discord in the area. Even where aid has been sincerely given in the hope of physically benefiting the people, there have been frustrations and setbacks, often caused by the limited Western understanding of Eastern people and their values. Typical is the Laotian village that was a recipient of a massive agricultural aid program. When the village was revisited the following year by aid officials to see how things were going, the headman explained the abandoned fields by observing, "You showed us how to double our crop last year, so there's no need for us to work this season." In spite of the gap in understanding, however, in the long haul there is no other way than by massive aid to dispel the poverty that is the breeding ground for communism.

The best the United States can do for Southeast Asia, India, and for the rest of the Third World is to give honest assistance where it is needed. At best, living standards can be upgraded. With the elimination of the poverty and ignorance that permit suppression of individuals under totalitarian forms of government, whether of the right or left, a freer, more open way of life may be expected. This may seem vague and uninspired counsel for the Western democracies, but there is consolation in the fact that the Communists, with all their concise dogma, have met with frustrations, too. Typical was the third Afro-Asian solidarity conference held in Tanzania under the very shadow of Mount Kilimanjaro. The hope was the harmonization of a Communist front in the Third World. The meeting was a failure. The delegates were in confusion, torn between Russia's talk of coexistence and disarmament and China's endorsement of revolution. On the third day of the conference, Kenya's delegate, Oginga Odinga, striving for concert, was driven to proclaim that the Sino-Soviet split was an invention of Western imperialism. Worse was to come. The Indian delegate finally walked out after a dispute with China over Tibet, declaring, "This conference is killed, ruined, finished; without India there is no conference." No one arose to dispute the point, and perhaps the conclusion applies in general to the situation of communism in the Third World.

Communism in the Americas

The United States Communism in the United States has had a long but frustrated history. Some of the party's intermediate objectives have been realized over a period of years, although usually through the efforts of noncommunists. The party's primary objective, however—the complete communization of the country—seems less likely now than when the first militant Marxist stepped off an immigrant ship in 1850.

American communism predates even Karl Marx. The ideology's first serious advocate in this country was George Rapp. Like Marx, Rapp was German, and he had read and taken to heart the Bible's fourth chapter of *Acts:* "And the multitude of them that believed were of one heart and one soul: neither said any of them that ought of the things he possessed was his own; but they had all things in common." Convinced of a communistic millennium to come, Rapp moved to the United States in 1803, bringing a congregation with him. This group had given all their property, real and personal, to Rapp and his associates for the benefit of the community, and in return they were guaranteed all the necessities of life. Should they ever desire to withdraw from the group, all their wealth would be returned. Thus was born Harmony, located in Indiana. The community was augmented later by an Englishman, Robert Owen, who after initiating industrial reform in his own factories, became a Utopian socialist. Unlike Rapp, Owen considered religion a superstition. He and his more worldly group eventually bought out Rapp at the Indiana settlement, for the German found the neighborhood attitudes unbearable. Owen renamed the community New Harmony. In the course of time the colony failed, due largely to friction over the theory of equal compensation irrespective of effort or productivity.

Before the demise of New Harmony, Marxist communism had made an enthusiastic if tentative appearance in the United States. Karl Marx himself took much interest in the Civil War, which he saw as a struggle against human bondage. On President Lincoln's reelection, Marx sent him a congratulatory letter that read in part:

> From the very beginning of the titanic American strife, the workers of Europe instinctively felt that the star-spangled banner carried the destiny of their class. . . . The workers of Europe feel sure that, as the American war of Independence initiated a new era of ascendancy for the middle class, so the American war against slavery will do it for the working class.

By this time Joseph Weydemeyer, another Marxist who had arrived in New York with the German immigrant flood of the early 1850s, had found there weren't enough readers for his Marxist magazine, *Die Revolution.* Undiscouraged, he went on to establish the small American Working Men's League, which campaigned against child labor and called for a guaranteed wage. He also sought compulsory education for children too poor to pay for it, as well as state tuition-free colleges. Unrealistic goals at the time, they had become standard practice within a century.

During the 1870s what had been a foreign-born, essentially foreign-speaking, movement began to attract native adherents with startling and party-splitting results. Rather stodgy German Marxists found themselves asked to support Victoria Woodhull, an eccentric women's rightist, for president. Her advocacy of free love was for many the last straw.

Marxism and American labor didn't really come to grips until 1890, when Daniel De Leon, a Dutch colonial born in Curaçao, joined the Socialist Labor party in New York. He gained influence in the Knights of Labor just in time to see that powerful labor union fade away, but he remained undaunted.

The year 1902 brought inspiration with the Pennsylvania coal strike. For the first time, organized labor successfully blocked a strategic industry for months without being condemned as a revolutionary menace. De Leon sensed the time was ripe for new radical leadership, and in 1905 he succeeded in taking over a newly formed Chicago labor organization. Made up of several groups too radical for the American Federation of Labor, this revolutionary combination called itself the Industrial Workers of the World. In time it became known as the IWW or "Wobblies." De Leon's efforts, however, to convert it to Marxism failed, and he was ousted.

De Leon was the last of the serious pre-Russian revolutionary socialists. When the American Communist party was founded in 1919, it was Russian-oriented. The German and American radical past was completely forgotten. Out of the night of World War I a new day was dawning, and the brightness came only from the East. It was a stormy day, full of strikes and labor unrest. In fact, the war had strengthened American capitalism, and the unrest was less a stirring of an attempt to overthrow the system than a revelation of a desire on labor's part to squeeze out more benefits for themselves. Still, the Communists were largely blamed, and the government-sanctioned crackdown drove the two branches of the party, one mostly foreign-born and Russian-oriented, the other native-born and more naturally democratic, into the underground. This outlawing of the party made it easier for American Communists to identify with Russian Bolshevism, and the native elements were absorbed into the Comintern.

However loudly the Comintern professed equality between national parties, the Soviet Union was predominant from the start. With the rise of Stalin, communism everywhere became subservient to the dictates of Russia. This has been a heavy cross, which the American party has borne with difficulty throughout its existence.

Stalin's hard-left revolutionary turn at the Sixth World Congress in 1928, a move responsive solely to Russia's internal affairs, left the American party foundering, a state from which it was rescued by the economic depression and Hitler's rise to power. The dreary combination suggested the decay of capitalism and seemed to hold out communism as a new faith for all men. Workers and unemployed housewives increased the party ranks in the early thirties, although the movement remained a weak one. At the Seventh World Congress, the Comintern about-faced and took up the United Front of democracy against fascism. Party membership reached 100,000. From the denunciation of bogus American democracy, the party switched to a new slogan, "Through Democracy to Socialism." American Communists became obsessed with the civil war in Spain. Many were recruited into that struggle, and many, it was said, learned to die before they learned to fight. These were the pure, heroic idealists. They would not appear again as lifeblood for the American Communist party.

That fascism prevailed in Spain was only the first of countless disillusioning shocks to come. Mother Russia's cynical military pact with Nazi Germany in 1939 left the American party limp and confused. Justifying the pact as a consequence of French and British treachery was more than most American Communists could swallow. Nor did glossing over it help, as Molotov did when he remarked to Ribbentrop, Germany's Foreign Minister, "Ideology is only a matter of taste." Still, a dedicated core rallied, called for labor strikes against American mobilization, and shouted, "The Yanks aren't coming." Right up until June 21, 1941, American Communists were busily organizing a National Peace Week. The next day, Germany invaded Russia. Peace Week died, to be replaced by American People's Mobilization Week. The pressure to strike was immediately replaced by a demand for an eighty-hour work week. Such opportunism left a bad smell that to some extent evaporated after Pearl Harbor. Before the war ended, "Meadowlands," as sung by the Red Army Chorus, had made the Hit Parade, and the darkly sinister Stalin had become just plain "Uncle Joe" who marched shoulder to shoulder with Uncle Sam.

Under the wartime leadership of Earl Browder, most American Communists came to imagine this bond between the United States and the USSR would be a permanent one. It was not to be. Once the war ended, the world promptly divided: the Free versus the Slave world, in American terminology; imperialist warmongers versus peace-loving Communists, if one preferred Soviet verbiage. Earl Browder, who had given the party an American image during the war, was branded a revisionist and cast out. William Foster, an old hard-liner who favored the class struggle, took his place.

Difficult days lay ahead. In the early 1950s, the intensifying cold war led to a host of Communist trials in the United States. Conviction no longer depended on an actual attempt to overthrow the government, but simply upon whether Communists had agreed (that is, conspired) to teach the overthrow of the government. This crime, which was defined by the Smith Act in 1941, was twice removed from actual violence. Under such pressure the party members, relying on the motto "Better fewer, but better," contracted to a dedicated core and went underground again. The storm raged above them and was spread by Senator Joseph McCarthy's investigations far beyond the bounds of communism. University professors, trade unionists, Jews, atheists, liberals, socialists, and "nonconformists" in general were attacked. In an atmosphere of fear and repression the testimony of former Communists such as Whittaker Chambers was used against officials like Alger Hiss. The conviction of the Rosenbergs of wartime conspiracy to spy for Russia led to their execution. McCarthy described his effort as "the fight for America." The fruits of these investigations, so far as finding an antigovernment plot, were nil. No more evidence was turned up than the FBI already had in its files. With the return to sanity, there were those in Washington who thought that McCarthy's disruption and degradation of American government had temporarily achieved results that went beyond Communist hopes.

Though American communism had weathered the federal trials and had scarcely been touched by McCarthy's inquiries, a near mortal blow was soon to follow. It came from within, at a time when convicted party members were being freed from jail and the party was returning to the surface. Cold-war antagonisms were easing. The American Communist party seemed on the verge of a second springtime when Stalin was denounced. He had been the oracle and the refuge in every calamity, the source of blind faith in moments of despair. The crisis was far more profound in the United States than in Europe, where the movement was a functioning part of the working class. In the United States, the party drew its strength primarily from idealists and intellectuals who now saw their convictions blown away.

By 1957, three factions attended the Communist national party convention. William Foster's far-left Stalinist group was doomed from the start. On the other hand, a group clustered behind John Gates, publisher of the *Daily Worker,* the Communist party newspaper. These, generally, were New York intellectuals who wanted the right to think for themselves now that the old dogmas were discarded. It was the same feeling that led to revolt in Poland and Hungary. It was equally unsuccessful and caused massive resignation and a weakening of the party from which it has never recovered.

Only the middle-of-the-roaders, behind Eugene Dennis, survived. Today the party is reduced in membership to some ten thousand. It continues under the leadership of Gus Hall, its Minnesota-born general secretary. Though hard-line in that it repudiates that recent heresy, Euro-Communism, it has again become almost respectable. With headquarters at 23 West 26th Street in New York City, it dutifully publishes the *Daily Worker* and suffers from the most damning realization in its history: it has become dull and old-fashioned.

The labor movement has simply passed it by. Unions need no advice from Moscow. They have their own muscle. So has the American black. Back in 1925, the blacks seemed the best Communist bet in the United States, and an "American Negro Labour Congress" was established. In 1932 a black, James Ford, ran for Vice-President on the Communist ticket. Most of his votes came from whites. The majority of blacks called him "Red Uncle Tom," and in this label lies the key to Communist failure with his group. Like the African of today, the American black doesn't want to be used. He has his own organizations, from the moderate NAACP to the radical Black Panthers. This growing militancy on the part of younger blacks raised Communist hopes. It was with a war whoop of joy that the American party leapt to the legal defense of Angela Davis, a glamorous black teacher and professed communist, who was accused of supplying weapons that were subsequently used to commit murder. But even these melodramatics attract few blacks, who, on the average, are "bourgeois" at heart. They want what the white man already has—property and economic power.

A more recent and seemingly fertile field for recruitment in the United States has been the college campus. There, the Communist activity of the new intellectual left centered in the Students for a Democratic Society. The hope was to move students' views from liberal to anticapitalist, from reform to revolution, but there were difficulties. The SDS adopted not only the red Communist flag but the black of anarchism and nihilism, offering no replacement for the existing order. Traditionally, Marxists and anarchists are bitter enemies, and what communism desires is controlled revolution, not guerrilla warfare. Now the SDS is defunct, with its leadership disillusioned, in jail or in hiding, and American communism is left groping for somewhere to go.

Latin America   More than any other continent containing several independent states, Latin America shares a common heritage. It was colonized by Portugal and Spain, Latin countries of similar culture. Theirs are the two principal languages spoken, and there is one Catholic religion throughout. Popular revolution during the nineteenth century achieved independence from Europe but generally left in control a Europeanized aristocracy that held the land with military support. The mass of peasants—native Indians, ex-African slaves, and mixed bloods—lived in semiservitude.

This opposition of rich versus poor with the catalyst of an emerging intelligentsia seemed, after World War I, to offer a tempting Communist target. Marx had shown no interest in South America, even though his son-in-law, Paul Lafargue, had been born in Cuba. The first radical ideas were introduced by immigrant workers in the mid-nineteenth century. There were more anarchists than Marxists among them. Official communism arrived only after World War I: in 1918 in Argentina, three years later in Chile, and four years after that in Cuba. These organizations were small, dissent-riven, and quite unable to keep abreast of upheavals within Russia. The confusion drove party leader Luis Emilio Recabarren to suicide in Chile, while in Cuba the party's founder, Julio Antonio Mella, was assassinated. Only since World War II has communism in Latin America borne anything but bitter fruit.

Mexico Unlike the Communist party in the United States, the party in Mexico has generally been allowed to operate in the open without stigma. The fact is that there are, to the detriment of communism in general, two competitive parties: the original Mexican Communist party and the People's party of 1948, which operates now under the name Partido Popular Socialista, and which absorbed the very small Mexican Worker-Peasant party in 1963. In terms of practical results, the Mexican Communists have shared in the United States' failure, but for different reasons.

The principal cause for their lack of success was timing. The Communists came too late. Mexico had already endured its bloody revolution, which began in 1910. The emerging government had its ear to the ground for malcontents. It gave concessions, removed unpopular governors, and adjusted wages before trouble could get out of hand. This alertness, coupled with general faith in the good life to come from the established Mexican system, provided barren ground for subversion. This is not to say that the Communist party has failed to make a sincere effort since its establishment in 1919. Its founder was an Indian nationalist, Manabendra Nath Roy, who had studied at Stanford University in the United States. He got into trouble, and from trouble into jail. From there, he fled to Mexico.

Initially, efforts were made to influence organized labor, without success. The Mexican peasants were isolated, unpolitical, and hard to recruit. In the end, party control fell entirely to intellectuals, and particularly to artists. The support of famous painters such as Diego Rivera, David Alfaro Sigueiros, and José Orozco gave Mexican communism publicity beyond its actual strength.

Since 1929 political power in Mexico has rested in the official government party, called, since 1946, the Institutional

Revolutionary party. In the late 1930s, under President General Lázaro Cárdenas, social, economic, and educational reforms were undertaken. Gradually the army was eased out of politics, while the government bureaucracy grew enormously. The business community has enlarged its political influence, changing the revolution's original goal of dividing up the economic cake into one of making the cake bigger.

The army as a creation of the revolution has never objected to nonmilitary tasks, such as dealing with unruly students or with restless political parties should they show signs of operating outside the accepted political framework. Other factors standing in the way of Communist growth in Mexico are the strong Catholic church and a culture that is basically Western in attitude. The great revolutionary hero Benito Juárez, though a full-blooded Zapotec Indian, succeeded less because of his blood than because he was a lawyer and statesman educated in the Western tradition. Nor is the anticolonial argument as persuasive as it is in Africa or the Arab world, for Mexico threw off all Spanish and French connections over a hundred years ago. Although the United States may at times be feared or envied, Mexico's political problems for the last several generations have been her own, and thus far she has provided adequate solutions.

In fact, the government is now so stable that the Communists in Mexico have been given wide freedoms, encouraged, perhaps, by Mexico's own revolutionary memories, which show a blend of liberalism and socialism. So long as any party "plays the game," there is no trouble. This means accepting the government, with criticisms limited to specific persons and actions, refraining from interference in foreign policy, and making no links with foreign governments. To overstep these limits is an invitation to the police and the army. Otherwise, the Communists are free to publish and free to use Mexico as a political haven, as many United States' Communists did during the conspiracy trials of the 1950s—as Trotsky had done before them. At present, Mexico is economically healthy, and the Institutional Revolutionary party shows no signs of losing dominance. Leftist guerrilla groups continue to operate in the hinterlands, but they are little more than bandits of the old school. Unless there is a drastic failure of the Mexican economy, the resident Communists, whether by bullet or ballot, would seem to have poor prospects in the foreseeable future.

Central America   Honduras, El Salvador, Nicaragua, Guatemala, Panama, and Costa Rica make up the six small nations of Central America. In the past they have been known contemptuously as the "banana republics" because U.S. banana growers wielded such influence among them. All remain poor, underdeveloped and subject to political upheaval. Such conditions are ripe for Communist insurrection. In 1948 Costa Rica came close to experiencing a communist dictatorship that was thwarted by a revolution staged by José Figueres Ferrer. More highly educated than its neighbors, Costa Rica has since achieved a working democracy. The others have not tended to be that fortunate. While democracy has not been achieved, neither has communism. The usual script calls for the threat of communism, real or imagined, followed by a military takeover, which is as likely to be simply a tyrannical excuse to seize power as a move to block the left. A good example was Nicaragua in the summer of 1978 where President Anastasio Samoza maintained bloody control of the small country with support from the National Guard. Those in opposition included guerrillas of a wide political persuasion. Even the Catholic Church called for Samoza's ouster, but thus far he has managed to "save the country" for himself and his soldiers. In 1954 Guatemala was drifting toward a Communist dictatorship under President Guzmán Jacabo Arbenz until the CIA intervened. Six years later, Honduras experienced a pro-Castro military seizure of power that promised socialist reforms, only to be ousted by another military group. In the same year the army in El Salvador supplanted a ruling clique of rich families known as the "Big Fourteen." Immediately another group of officers accused them of being "soft on communism" and took over. They have since surprised everyone by nationalizing the country's Central Reserve Bank and by allowing truly democratic elections. More recently the focus has been on Panama, due to the negotiations for the United States to eventually surrender con trol of the canal to that country. Needless to say, the United States' military presence there over the years has made for hostility. Many Panamanians openly admire Castro and his revolution, and it is the old fear of communist revolution, not entirely without justification, which made for a stiff congressional dissent before the treaty could be ratified.

Cuba Communism's most spectacular victory in Latin America has come in Cuba, which, in point of fact, was more inheritance than victory. The leader in the revolt was Fidel Castro. Born in 1927 in Oriente Province, Castro was educated in Santiago and Havana and received his law degree at Havana University in 1950. Three years later, his attack on the military barracks in Santiago de Cuba touched off a resistance of disgruntled, land-hungry peasant farmers against the dictator Batista, who was supported by the big estate owners. By 1958, this old regime was on the run. Robin Hood had bested the Sheriff of Nottingham, and most Americans applauded. Cuban as well as international Communists had been taken by surprise. They were of the older urban industrial school of Russian Communists. Castro and his followers, though they may not have realized it at the time, had followed more closely the Chinese pattern of revolution.

The official Communist party of Cuba had gotten off to an early start in 1925. Russia gave the directives, but the impressive resistance of the Chinese Communist Army against the Kuomintang did not go unnoticed. The political opponents chosen by the Cuban Communists were not the establishment, but those parties which competed for dominance of the political left: reformers, anarchists, Trotskyites. These might steal Communist fire, while, hopefully, the establishment would provide a ripe and useful target for orthodox Communist revolution. With this in mind, Fulgencio Batista was supported enthusiastically in his rise to dictatorial power. The orthodox Communists were right to the extent that Batista created excellent cause for a revolution, but by the time Castro had decided that Russia was a more desirable ally than the United States, the old Cuban Communist party was out of a job. Batista fled the country January 1, 1959. Many refugees were to follow him. These unhappy exiles, concentrated in Florida, attempted an invasion of Cuba with surreptitious aid from the United States. This 1961 fiasco was firmly put down by the Cubans at the Bay of Pigs.

Fidel Castro is no theoretical Communist. He has shown scorn for philosophers who tend to overlook practical problems, particularly since the removal of the militant Che Guevara from the Cuban scene. Many of Castro's pragmatic programs have shown positive results. A vigorous campaign to enlist "people's teachers" was instituted under the slogan "The people will teach the people." This program has done much to enhance the quantity if not the quality of education. Lessons for the illiterate, two hours a day after working hours, begin with a fifteen-lesson primer entitled *Venceremos* ("We shall conquer"). Once the student can read this book and can write a letter to Fidel saying so, he will, ideally, move on to more advanced work.

The Cuban Revolution was dedicated to far-reaching reforms, and the rest of Latin America has shown an inclination to try the same path. In Cuba, property owned by the United States was seized, and all large private enterprises were nationalized in the usual manner. Landholdings were cut to a maximum of 1,000 acres with the surplus going to renters, sharecroppers, and peasants. Later, the maximum private acreage was cut to 167 acres. Still, individual farmers managed to survive and to hold 45 percent of the land, selling their produce on the free market at a price above the official prices. The state needs these farmers' support, for their farms operate more efficiently than the state-run farms, which at present cannot alone meet the demands.

The problem with the latter is incentive. The Cuban peasant is used to being driven mercilessly. Formerly, the impetus was fear of starvation. That fear has now been removed, but positive incentives are few. As yet, no physical coercion has been applied. But the voluntary mobilization of the youth into semi-military work forces is proving far from a successful answer, particularly when the national fervor that at first accompanies popular revolution is bound to be on the wane. For the time being, however, such mobilization remains a useful device. It has been particularly successful on the Isle of Pines, rechristened the Isle of Youth, where thousands of young people live collectively, working on the state citrus groves.

Meanwhile, the independent farmer subsists. Since the state still needs him, there is no threat of his farm being taken by fiat. However, over the long haul the regime has devised a policy of attrition to eliminate him. Though his son may inherit his farm, his land may not be sold, and where there is no heir, the state confiscates the property. An inducement to encourage collectivization of farm land is the government offer of a furnished house complete with television in exchange for the farmer's private holdings. Other restrictive regulations kept farmers from a wholesale market by a limitation on the purchase in the free market to 24 pounds (10.8 kg) in bulk. Motorized private transportation has virtually disappeared, which inhibits marketing. The upgrading of produce in state stores is expected, and this will contribute to the elimination of demands on the free market.

Private ownership outside of agriculture has been drastically curtailed. While major industries were immediately appropriated by the state, small private enterprises such as bars and food shops resisted until 1968. Then over 57,000 small businesses were nationalized, and their former owners were screened for other employment, usually agricultural. Left out of this mass appropriation were only the owners of private trucks and cabs, whose businesses cannot outlast the life of their fast-deteriorating equipment. The main reason for this drastic step of nationalization, of course, was to put an end to the demoralizing effect of private enterprises on a public otherwise dependent on the state.

Post-Revolution Cuba was slow to assert itself in foreign affairs. It was not until 1961 that Castro announced his conversion to Marxism-Leninism. A few months later, with his second Havana Declaration, he set forth a blueprint for the exportation of the Cuban system to the rest of Latin America, a kind of Latin American Communist manifesto that called for revolution first and then communism to follow. This doctrine failed to recognize that, despite anti-Yankeeism in South America, that continent has many strong Western cultural links. Latin American Communists may speak of the "glorious Cuban Revolution," but they still reject Castro's bloody methods and resent his criticism. Most South American Communists, also being nationalists, do not want the help of agents outside their countries and have informed Castro that he is not "the pope of Revolution."

In the autumn of 1962, the construction of Soviet missile bases in Cuba led to another dangerous confrontation, this time between Russian supply ships and American naval vessels. Fortunately, the Russians agreed to remove the rocket launchers, and the crisis passed. The result was a humiliation for Premier Khrushchev and the warming of Cuban-Chinese relations, an additional affront to the Soviet Union.

Communist China, along with Che Guevara, remained prominent in Cuban politics during Castro's active campaign to export violent revolution to South America. Che Guevara was the romantic personification of insurrection and a bit too much for Castro himself to handle. Guevara's departure to South America must have brought a sigh of relief to many Cubans, and his death there, while loudly lamented, surely caused that sigh to be repeated. Like Guevara, China held brief sway in Cuba. As the clamor for revolution subsided, the Maoists were accused of trying to strangle the Cuban economy while at the same time subverting the army. Reliance shifted back to the Soviets. Russian technicians and industrial aid will be a fixture of Cuban life as long as Castro remains a compliant host and the Cuban economy requires Soviet bolstering. Cuban support for the invasion of Czechoslovakia in 1968 was gratifying to the Russians, and in the mid-1970s Cuba assumed a growing role as Moscow's agent in Black Africa. By the autumn of 1977, about 25,000 Cuban soldiers and civilians had flooded into a dozen African countries, the majority concentrated in Angola and Ethiopia. Without Cuban support the Communist regime would undoubtedly topple, and Castro is adamant in his resolve to keep his "technicians" there. The result is a roadblock in the path of renewed United States-Cuban trade. Until the Angolan adventure, prospects had seemed good for improved relations between the United States and Cuba, and the latter would very much like to exchange her surplus sugar for agribusiness equipment and computer technology.

Cuba's prospects are mixed. Politically, the island is stable, largely owing to Castro's personality. He is still beloved and revered. Economically, progress has been disappointing. Diet remains austere with most foods rationed, clothing is scarce, and consumer goods, which Castro refers to as junk and trinkets, are nonexistent. Without much to buy, excess private funds are skimmed off at the few good restaurants such as the old Floredita, one of Ernest Hemingway's favorites, where a lobster dinner goes for about 40 dollars a person. Government reserves, such as they are, have largely gone toward education, health care, and housing, but 86 percent of Cuba's foreign earnings come from sugar exports, and in 1976 sugar sank from 60 to 7 cents per pound (.45 kg). Though slightly recovered, Cuba remains five billion dollars in debt to the Soviet Union for oil, electric power, and farm and industrial equipment. While the Cuban people are used to a paternalistic government, the wild enthusiasm that got the revolution off to a good start has already begun to lag. Cuban communism set impossible goals for itself. Where moral incentives had been thought, in the 1960s, to be sufficient to motivate workers, by the mid-1970s a new economic management and planning system pushed managers to raise earnings over costs, with the surplus to be distributed to workers directly or put into social improvements such as day-care centers. The threat from without, which has sustained many an embattled nation, has also disappeared. Invasion from the United States is no longer expected. The Cuban Revolution has passed its emotional peak, and the new threat of decay from within is being met in the usual totalitarian form. The communistic party bureaucracy has begun to harden. Artistic and literary freedom have vanished, and there is rigid insistence on the official view. The recent government move against poet Heberto Padillo was a case in point. As long as Castro remains strong, his programs will be followed, however limpingly. What will happen if he weakens is beyond prediction.

Chile The only other Latin American country to experiment with a Socialist Marxist government was Chile. Theoretically, unlike other Communist countries, political changeover was achieved by democratic election, without benefit of outside interference or subversion. Since the days of her own revolution in 1817 when Spain's colonial regime was overthrown, Chile has been fiercely independent. A typical story reflecting the spirit of the people is that of a captain in the rebel cause whose shattered arm had just been amputated. He returned to the fray with the severed limb held on high, shouting, "Viva La Patria!"

For almost three hundred quiet years, the country was a minor province under Spanish control. The drive for independence began in Chile during the Napoleonic Wars. The country's first ruler, Bernardo O'Higgins, was committed to the ideals of representative government and democracy. To this end, he forbade the use of titles and coats of arms, and he tried to foster a small farmer class at the expense of the *mayorazgos*, the large landholders. Here he was in trouble, for the aristocracy joined with the conservative clergy and forced O'Higgins to abdicate. By 1833, the landed interests had won out, and the right to vote was limited to the literate and well-to-do. This set the pattern of restricted prosperity that is behind Chile's present upheavals.

Throughout the following century, the government remained stable. Reforms were slowly adopted and there developed in the people of Chile a great respect for law and order and an expectation of social reforms within the governmental structure. Indicative of this unique orderliness in Chile are the sidewalk vendors of the latest laws. Their cry is, "A law for today, Señor," and the citizens buy the printed copies with avid interest.

During the 1920s, a Communist party developed in Chile and received much support of an intellectual nature. In 1948, at a time when Russia was first becoming interested in Latin America, the party was briefly declared illegal. For a time, particularly during U.S. President John F. Kennedy's Alliance for Progress program, the Communists seemed to lose ground.

More popular was the newly emergent Christian Democratic party, which called for "revolution with freedom."

Unfortunately, Chile's economic crisis is almost beyond political solution. Her national economy has always depended upon one major export. Until the end of World War I, it was nitrates, with the business largely in British hands. Subsequently, it has been copper, with the United States taking charge. The decline of one cent per pound (.45 kg) in the price of copper in the world market means that Chile loses 15 million dollars in annual revenue. Such helpless dependency on foreign business interests produced agitation for the nationalization of industry long before the Communists took over the government. Then Chile began to nationalize the copper mines owned by the American firms of Anaconda and Kennecott, without repayment. A low profit margin brought continued economic crisis.

While the national economy of Chile is dominated by foreign interests, land ownership has long been concentrated in the hands of a small Chilean elite. The work is done by tenant farmers feudally dependent on their patron for food, clothing, and protection. This economic stranglehold began to break up with the enlargement of the working middle classes. They banded together against the political tyranny of the aristocracy in 1920, and their Liberal Alliance candidate, Arturo Alessandri, was elected president. He achieved much reform legislation, but it was insufficient to keep pace with mounting social and economic problems. The rich landowners still controlled 86 percent of the arable land, and the rural population of Chile, about one-third of the total population, remained poverty ridden. Urban workers fared little better, for wages have never kept up with the fearful inflation. From 1940 to 1950 prices rose over 400 percent, and from 1950 to 1960, over 2,000 percent. Even public servants often subsist on one meal a day, and the consequence of such impossible inflation has been to attract not only the working but the middle class to the far left.

By 1958 the Alliance party, led by Alessandri's son, Jorge Alessandri Rodriguez, barely won by 30,000 votes over a

Marxist-backed Socialist-Communist coalition, and, six years later, his party was not even in the race. Opposing the extreme left was Eduardo Frei, a Christian Democrat, whose program was scarcely less radical than that of the Communists. Frei won, and proposed a "revolution with freedom." The goal was to be one of raising the country's material condition, not in the paternalistic manner, but in such a way as to promote human values. Fine words, but difficult of achievement. A large population increase was causing an urban drift. Shantytowns—autonomous villages, self-governed and aggressively independent—were everywhere. Industrialization was needed to broaden the economic base, but about 25 percent of the citizens lived at a bare subsistence level, and there was no market in the country for manufactured goods.

During his term of office, Frei successfully increased copper production, but all the while his Christian Democrats were under challenge from the right and left. It was more like a workers' strike than a rebellion when some of the Chilean Army mutinied in 1969 for more pay. Though the economy was growing, so were problems, and Frei's six-year term was running out. He could not succeed himself, and the Christian Democrats could offer no satisfactory successor. On the other hand, the Communist-Socialist alliance put forward Salvador Allende Gossens, a fiery Socialist-Marxist, and the neat formula of Marxism seemed to offer a plan, an ideology, and the plausible answer to all problems. The Christian Democratic vote was nibbled away by a rightist law-and-order party led by former president Jorge Alessandri Rodriguez. Allende came out the winner in September, 1970, with 36 percent of the votes cast.

Allende was an avowed Marxist, but not a Communist in the traditional sense. For one thing, he disclaimed the necessity of revolution to bring about social change. However, the Communist party of Chile was one of the major groups in his Popular Unity coalition party. New agrarian reform laws limited individual holdings in Chile to 176 acres (70 hectares) of irrigated land or 600 acres (240 hectares) of nonirrigated pasture. Where change moved too slowly, peasants seized estates illegally, but most Chileans retained respect for law and order. Simon Bolívar, nineteenth-century hero of South American liberation, had held out hope for Chile when he said, "If any republic is to last a long time in America, I think it will be that of Chile. . . . Chile can be free."

It was not for Allende to fulfill this prediction. On September 11, 1973, following a period of paralyzing strikes, economic chaos, cabinet crisis, and street brawling, a military junta led by General Augusto Pinochet Ugarte demanded President Allende's resignation. Allende, by radio broadcast, refused. The Chilean Air Force strafed his palace, took it by assault, and found Allende dead, as was his dream of democratic Marxist-Socialism. Subsequently the military leaders formed a fifteen-man cabinet with Ugarte as the president. They vowed to "exterminate Marxism" throughout Chile and to expel the allegedly more than 10,000 foreign "extremists" to whom Allende had given refuge. Thousands were arrested, many were summarily executed. Relations with Cuba were cut while foreign investment in mining was again encouraged, and claims were settled with companies that Allende had nationalized. The goal, of course, was to curb runaway inflation and reinstate international business, with the end product being a form of capitalistic corporate state along the lines once favored by Mussolini in Italy. The present cost is a 20 percent unemployment rate and a recession, but there remains substantial support for General Pinochet, as evidenced by a 77 percent vote of national confidence in January 1978, supporting him against a United Nations' condemnation of his regime's violations of human rights. Today one more South American "military trusteeship" seems firmly in place.

Political Alternatives in Latin America Throughout Latin America, a certain amount of polarization has taken place since the Alliance for Progress days of the early 1960s. Of the 280 million Latin Americans, about half live under right-wing military governments, less than one in ten under Marxist-Socialism, and the rest under governments that wobble uncertainly in between. The landowners, big business, the church hierarchy, and—in most cases—the army, stand on one side; the growing mass of the underprivileged rank on the other.

In Brazil, for example, 3 percent of the nation's 90 million people own 62 percent of the land. Eighty-two percent of South American industry is owned by U.S. capitalists, and yet these North American investors, however resented, employ 2 million South American workers, pay one-fifth of the taxes, and produce one-third of the exports. Without them, the economy would collapse.

The shaky democracies of the early 1960s were simply not up to the massive job of effecting the needed change in the continent's life. A Communist surge from the bottom would probably fare no better. In June of 1970, Argentina's president, former General Juan Carlos Ongania, was removed from office by a military junta. Most citizens ignored the affair, saying, "This is a military matter. What have politics to do with me?" This is a common attitude in the area and suggests a solution that may be more likely than communism to prevail in Latin America. The military strong man has long been a familiar figure. The tradition goes back to Símon Bolívar and José de San Martin, who drove Spain out of the land. Most South American military regimes are convinced, with reason, that the civilian politicians are corruptible and incompetent, and there are many examples where military groups have made acceptable improvements. One of these was the predominantly neofascist government of Argentina when Perón and his Peronistas took political power from the aristocracy. They put power not only into their own hands, but into those of the middle and working classes as well.

Other military cliques have been composed of dedicated young officers. Such was the group that came to power in 1968 in Peru under General Juan Velasco Avarado. With the intent of strengthening the position of the state in order to bring changes for the better, many large foreign holdings in the country were expropriated. Some middle-class and upper-class people have been forced to leave. But if anything is to be done to rectify the swelling poverty of the masses, there may be no better course at present than this new military socialism.

In Bolivia, General Juan José Torres followed a similar path until his overthrow in August 1971. In Brazil, the Escola Superior Guerra, modeled after Washington's War College, has not only concerned itself with matters of war, revolution, and prevention of foreign subversion, but it has undertaken the study of economics and sociology. The old image of the bandoliered, bemedaled autocrat has shifted to that of technical expert, very much concerned with the national future. In effect, it is a Latin American form of Nasserism.

The extreme alternative on the left, advocated less loudly now by Cuba's Castro, has been called Jacobin after a group in the French Revolution that would never compromise. Lenin used the term for those Communists who insisted irrevocably on the bloody revolution of the proletariat. Such is the implacable doctrine of the New Left in Latin America, which has turned its back on Soviet gradualism. The old-line political Communists are "establishment" and obsolete as far as these radicals are concerned. Characteristic were Uruguay's Tupamaros, a terrorist organization. It refused, or was perhaps intellectually unable, to define its political and revolutionary goals beyond bringing down the present system through bombings, burnings, and murder. Such an approach provides no long-term solution. Though Nasserism may seem a sad substitute for democracy, it is at least preferable to revolution for revolution's sake. From an objective point of view, it is about the best present alternative for the social crisis that confronts Latin America.

Conclusion:
The Emerging Future

When the sweet old lady who always had a kind word for everyone was asked to comment on Satan, she remarked, after a moment's hesitation, "Well, I certainly think he's hardworking." Though even the most conscientious red-baiter is no longer likely to equate the Devil with communism, the old lady's thought does suitably head a list of communism's strengths and virtues. In the material world, progress has been staggering. From preponderant illiteracy after World War I, Russia has moved to over 67 percent literacy. There are, per-capita, more doctors and engineers there than in the United States. Like Satan, communism measures its success in very materialistic terms, and herein lies their mutual sin against the human spirit. Both are powerful adversaries in the material world, but they will founder at the strength of a social order in which the ends of morality, individual free expression, and justice are served.

Thus far, communism has had its major successes in nations where the governments have been torn by war and where the mass of the population has been existing at near survival levels. Only where misery is rampant will a country surrender its measure of stability for the bloody hazard of revolution. This incendiary discontent, according to Marxian doctrine, was expected from the working class of factory laborers, but much has changed in the West since those early capitalistic days. Though Marx imagined the lot of these workers getting worse and worse as capitalistic profits were extracted at the expense of their wages, such projected inequities have been balanced out by the progressive income tax and the minimum wage.

Other factors Marx misjudged were the adaptability of the capitalist class and the growing power of trade unions. Theodore Roosevelt initiated the Square Deal; Woodrow Wilson, the New Freedom; Franklin D. Roosevelt, the New Deal; John Kennedy, The New Frontier; and Lyndon Johnson, the Great Society. All moved to give labor a stake in the system. Communism may label such measures, as they did on the rise of the British Labour party, clever plots on the part of big business to keep itself in power, by the fact remains that the exploited proletariat of the nineteenth century no longer exists. And even if the bulk of labor calls itself the Communist party, as in France, that does not make it a revolutionary force. The object is simply a strong voting voice to enhance their own material interests in the system as it exists.

The curious irony of present-day communism is, on the one hand, its failure to arouse the prospering workers of the world to revolution despite sharp increases in industrial expansion. On the other hand, communization of agriculture has been a uniform disappointment, and yet it is in agrarian countries that the Communist appeal still has revolutionary strength.

Industrial success has come very largely at the price of doctrine. In the early days of the Soviet Union, wage levels reflected the idea that all workers were comrades toiling together, and the spread of income from the lowest manual worker to the highest plant manager was no more than one to two. Now, with the grudging admission that men work for personal, not utopian goals, wages of some have been raised to the point where the spread is fifteen to one. That is not the only shift from theory toward capitalist reality. Planners have moved from the old command economy of the Stalinist era to the Western notion of an economy responsive to demand. The goal of gross production that made for shoddy goods and hoarding of material to meet quotas has given way to more autonomy of management at the factory level.

Individual enterprise has by no means vanished in many Communist countries. The best planning system leaves unavoidable gaps, and there is always someone to make pitch-forks or, should the demand exist, sell tropical fish. Farmers cling tenaciously to their land, and, where the opportunity avails, will farm independently at the expense of the coop-erative or collective. An extreme example of possessiveness occurred in Russia, where a farmer so cherished his small apple orchard that, to thwart marauding boys, he planted land mines. This sense of ownership and of belonging is hard to train away. Many psychologists would argue it is basic to human nature and, though the farmer in question stepped on one of his own mines and lost an eye for his trouble, a spirit like his is apt to cause orthodox Communists more, not less, trouble in years to come.

If this individualism is a threat to orthodox communism, its converse, bureaucratic conformity, is even more of a menace to the neocommunism of the future. Kosygin and Brezhnev wear gray flannel suits. Their revolutionary forefathers were great social innovators, but they represent an entrenched poli-tical orthodoxy that resists experimentation. Ideas from outside the Soviet Union are suspect. Any individualism or criti-cism, however constructive in intent, is frowned upon. Khrush-chev looked at modern art and commented with disgust that it had been "painted with a donkey's tail." The present regime has intensified the attack on arts and letters. Such closed totalitarianism cannot progress in a world where change is the only certainty.

A more obvious and constant stumbling block to the real-ization of Communist goals has been religion. As an atheist, Marx regarded religion simply as the "spiritual aroma" of a dying system; it was not worth a major attack. His followers have taken it more seriously as antirevolutionary, "the pus of a sick world," and one of the causes for the failures of the proletarian revolution. Communist doctrine predicted that sci-ence would eventually answer all questions and that a Com-munist paradise would replace a spiritual one. Superficially, communism has mimicked religion, particularly Catholicism. It is possible to point to similarities between the structure of the Vatican and the Kremlin. Original sin becomes private property; Marx, Lenin, and Stalin become Father, Son, and

Holy Ghost; paradise, the communist millennium. Whatever the similarities, religion answers one compelling question that communism never can: the question of human mortality. Without death, there would be little, if any, religion, but as long as that unattractive mystery persists, religion will have a following in the world at large as well as within the Communist sanctuaries.

Soviet policy has generally been to contain rather than eradicate religion. Many theological colleges have been closed and priests' licenses suspended, yet those churches that remain open are packed on Sundays. Clergymen, such as Cardinal Mindszenty of Hungary, have been jailed and persecuted for stepping outside the church into politics. In the long run, the contest is apt to remain a standoff. In such firmly religious countries as Poland, communism and religion have learned to get along together. There is no reason why practical communism with its ideologies softened cannot function in cooperation with Islam or the Christian church.

While Soviet Communism and the Christian church, though in conflict, show structural similarities, the mystique of Chinese communism can, in part, be explained from absorption of oriental religious traditions. Principally, these are Taoism, which stresses the meditative way to inner tranquility and enlightenment, and Confucianism, which exhorts that all intellectual and moral energy can be channeled for self-perfection, the common good, and social and universal peace. Here is no clash of monolithic institutions such as exists between the Russian party and the Church, but an adaptable, philosophic mold into which Maoism fits with ease.

In the former colonial areas of the world, communism has had to face another grave disappointment. Russia has always represented itself as the spearhead of the drive to overcome imperialism and colonialism. Now Western colonialism in its most conspicuous areas, Africa and Asia, has all but vanished, not, as the Communists hoped, by revolution, but by voluntary surrender. These new nations have their problems—social and political. Communism is only one of the solutions being applied, and not the most popular one at that. Meanwhile, Russia remains in the position of being the greatest colonial power on earth. While Britain and France were painfully severing their colonial relations, Russia was securing them in Georgia and Turkestan.

Turkestan is Russia's largest colony in Asia. Traditionally, it was a Muslim region, with its own identity. But under Soviet dominion it was divided up into national soviet republics and consequently vanished as an entity from Russian maps. Political leaders who resisted this absorption went to prison or before the firing squad. The Turkestan poet Cholpan wrote a poem to the Russian Communists: "Pack your suitcases, make Turkestan free." He, too, was shot. This duplicity, as well as China's absorption of Tibet, has not been lost on the non-aligned nations. They are also aware of Russia's actions in Hungary and Czechoslovakia. It is less likely that the future of world communism will be decided in Moscow, Peking, or Washington, D.C., than in such uncommitted capitals as Delhi, Brasilia, and Dar es Salaam.

Western democracies can give no single answer to communism. In a free society with an intellectual heritage of many philosophies, there must be many answers. Apart from any philosophy, there is one psychological fact ignored by communism in its obsession with economics. That factor is a sense of national belonging, ironical because Marx imagined communism could create a global community of workers that transcended other loyalties. Today that feeling is manifest in international terms as nationalism; and it ranges from the extremes of Gaullism down to the self-importance of the smallest emergent nation. Mother tongues and national cultures will prevail over Communist philosophy even as they have prevailed, when put to the test, in Russia and China.

Nationalism, more than anything else, has broken up the monolithic front that communism once presented to the world. The old objectives of world revolution can now, at best, be envisioned as individual national revolutions. And the Communist leaders of today cannot question that the old dream of a united struggle to the death against capitalism is a desperate one that would cost them far more than they are willing to pay.

There is a refreshing irony in this grudging realization, East and West, that both communism and democratic capitalism are apt to be around for a long time. It has developed into a limited adversary relationship between the Soviet Union and the United States. Formerly, communism waited on the thought that capitalism would vanish through pure economic logic. The United States hoped for a democratic counter-revolution in Russia. Both proved to be false hopes. Though the ultimate political expectations of these two countries may remain irreconcilable, this fact has tended to recede into the hazy future. Between the two countries have developed parallel, if not mutual, interests. Both have concern for growing nationalism in other parts of the world. Both are aware of the undesirability of the spread of nuclear weapons. The developing situation might even be called an alliance between two world powers against war between themselves. It does not mean an end to friction, but it does imply restraint: the United States in Hungary and in Cuba; Russia in Vietnam and in the Cuban missile crisis. The provocations are there if either country wants to use them. A prime example was the played-down opposition of American fighter pilots versus Soviet-operated missile bases in North Vietnam.

The goal of Communist world revolution is further away now than it was thirty years ago. Marxian doctrines have to a large extent been abandoned, but even if they never fitted the world situation, this philosophy must be given credit for inspiring the most major social change since the middle of the nineteenth century. Its impact endures even though its theories have not been specifically carried out. The philosophical goal of communism has always been admirable, but it seems no more attainable now than when it was conceived. For such a material paradise, incredible abundance is vital. No Communist country has come close to such requisite prosperity, though most have made very real progress from poverty to industrialization. For such a paradise, people must be inspired by different motives than are known in the West. They must have leaders of complete dedication and selflessness. Neither the Soviet Union nor China has molded such supermen, and they are not likely to in the foreseeable future. However, they have galvanized their nations into productive efforts formerly unimagined.

A true Communist society requires absolute equality among its members. Such equality is not part of the human condition and not part of existing Communist societies, where power seems just as sweet as it does anywhere else in the world. In an ideal Communist society, the people must be free, but this has been realized less than any other ideal by Communist governments. They remain, by and large, totalitarian and intolerant of individual expression or criticism.

Communism as it is practiced today can never lead to the Marxist millennium. In many ways it demands that people live contrary to their instincts. Like Crowell's Puritans, will it simply fade away because man reaches a point where he prefers comfort and entertainment to stern moral purpose? Probably not; but to survive, it must adjust to a changing world. It is to be hoped that with increasing stability, its totalitarian and embattled aspects will be laid aside.

Definitions

Alienation In Marxist usage this word signifies the situation in which capitalism has placed the working proletariat. Having been alienated from the profit structure the workers are then in a position to understand the mainsprings of society and with such enlightenment move ahead to take over the system, thereby putting an end to capitalism's repression, exploitation, and alienation.

Anarchism The political belief that all oppression comes from the state, which must be overthrown. Communists have always opposed the theory of anarchism.

Bolshevik Means in Russian, literally, "the majority." The word was first used by the Communists in 1903 when Lenin caused a split in the Russian Social Democratic Labor party over whether revolution should be achieved by democratic evolution or by violence. Lenin favored the latter course and won the support of the majority of the party for the seizure of power during the revolution. The term has become a synonym for "Communist." *See also* Menshevik.

Bourgeoisie In Communist terms, the social class that owns the means of production and can live on its resources without having to sell its labor to survive. Originally the French word had meant simply those who lived in towns.

Cadre The Communist party members who serve as a nucleus in their offices or institutions and are capable of training others in party functions. The Chinese party relies heavily on carefully indoctrinated cadres.

Centrism Marx's theory held that the communist revolution must pass through a bourgeois stage before socialism could develop. In his own words, "The industrially more developed country shows the less developed country only a picture of its own future . . . A society cannot skip over the natural phases of development, nor can it replace them by decrees." Dealing with the realities of revolution in Russia's essentially peasant culture, Lenin abandoned this step in his doctrine of revolution.

Class Struggle The conflict among economic groups in society that Marx believed was the cause of all social and historical change.

Classless society The unified social and economic existence that, in Communist thinking, is the final stage in history and thus the goal of communism. *See also* Millennium.

Collectivization The process of bringing land under the control of large state-owned and state-operated farms.

Cominform The Communist Information Bureau. Organized in 1947 for the purpose of bringing the Eastern European satellite countries and the Communist parties of France and Italy under the control of one semipolitical body and to aid in the spread of communism throughout the world. The Cominform was dissolved in 1956, three years after the death of Stalin.

Comintern The first truly international Communist convention, formally called the Third International. Organized in 1919, it guided the spread of international communism until the organization was dissolved in 1943. *See also* Internationals.

Commune A large state-run, involuntary unit into which Chinese peasants were organized during the Great Leap Forward of the late 1950s.

Cult of personality, or cult of the individual The aberration from Marxist doctrine that occurs when a leader sets himself up as an individual above Communist principles. In 1956 Khrushchev denounced Stalin's rule for its cult of personality.

Democratic centralism A term used by Lenin to indicate a combination of dictatorship with his idea of democracy, which actually meant mass participation in political activities.

Dialectical materialism A theory that explains the course of history in terms of the economic struggle that takes place between classes in society. The theory was developed by Marx and Engels, who based their thinking on the ideas of Hegel.

Exploitation A term used by Marx for the practice of taking from the worker labor of more value than is recompensed by his wages.

First International *See* Internationals.

Five-year plan Beginning in 1927, the Soviet Union established a series of economic plans that set objectives for industry and agriculture to be realized within the five-year scope of the plan.

Imperialism In Communist phraseology, the last stage of capitalism, in which free competition is replaced by monopoly.

Industrial Workers of the World (IWW) A labor group formed in 1905, nicknamed the Wobblies. The organizations' position was antiwar and tended toward communism.

Internationals The First International or the International Workingmen's Association was established in London by Marx and Engels in 1864 to link national workers' societies and further Marxian aims. The organization dissolved in 1876. The Second International, formed in 1889, was made up of socialist parties. For the Third International, *see* Comintern.

Jacobin In Marxist vocabulary the extremist group who insist on the rule of the revolutionary proletariat all the way to the dawn of communism. The term originally meant the extremist political group active in the French Revolution.

Kulak In Russian Communist terms, a prosperous peasant farmer who profited from the oppression of other farmers and resisted collectivization. In the 1930s large numbers of kulaks were liquidated.

Leap In the Marxist theory of history a "leap" is a break with gradual evolution, causing an abrupt emergence or a new reality.

Maoism Marxism as developed in China by Chairman Mao Tse-tung, placing emphasis on revolutionary peasantry rather than upon industrial workers. Mao contributed much to the idea of a people's war in which a conventional Red Army would cooperate with the people's guerrillas.

Menshevik Means in Russian, literally, "the minority." The word was first used by the Communists in 1903 in the split in the Russian Social Democratic Labor party over whether revolution should be achieved by democratic evolution or by violence. The Mensheviks believed in the evolutionary process. *See also* Bolshevik.

Millennium In Marxist phraseology, the ultimate classless society marked by a maximum of human goodness and cooperation maintained without the control of governmental apparatus. *See also* Classless society.

Party line The positions taken and tactics endorsed by the world Communist movement.

Politburo The policy-making and executive committee of a national Communist party.

Pravda Literally, "the truth." The official Soviet Russian newspaper.

Presidium The permanent committee that exercises executive power in a Communist country. The Soviet presidium is selected from the Supreme Soviet.

Proletariat Wage earners, in particular; industrial workers.

Revisionism In Communist terminology, the attempt to change the approach of communism from a revolutionary movement to one working by evolutionary means to achieve socialism.

Soviet In Russian, literally, "a council." Under communism the soviet became the fundamental unit of government. Revolutionary councils, or soviets, were first created in 1905 and were made up of factory workers. The government in Russia today rests upon a hierarchy of soviets. *See also* Supreme Soviet.

Supreme Soviet The highest body of governmental power in Soviet Russia, which elects the supreme court, the procurator-general, and the presidium. *See also* Presidium.

Surplus value The Communist term for a capitalist's profits. According to Marx, the difference between the actual value of a worker's labor, as determined by the market price of the product, and the amount the worker is paid in wages represents the surplus value, which the worker is denied and the capitalist takes as profit.

Trotskyism Specifically, the views of Trotsky, and generally, any deviation from the party line.

Vanguard The elite, the Communists, who lead the way to revolution.

Yezhovshchina The great Soviet purges of the late 1930s.

Biographies

Allende Gossens, Dr. Salvador (1908–1973). The son of a provincial Chilean lawyer, Allende studied medicine at the University of Chile. Helped found the Chilean Socialist party. He was first elected a national deputy in 1937 and became the first Marxist president in 1970. Deposed in 1973 and died in the upheaval, an apparent suicide.

Brezhnev, Leonid I. (1906–   ): Born in the Ukraine, he received a technical education and held various local engineering positions and political offices. From 1941 to 1946 Brezhnev was a political officer in the Soviet Army and subsequently began moving up through party ranks. Since 1966 General Secretary of the Communist party of the U.S.S.R. and also since 1977 President of the Supreme Soviet.

Castro, Fidel (1927–   ): Educated at Jesuit schools in Santiago and Havana, Cuba, and at Havana University, Castro began a law practice in Havana and became active in the political opposition to the Batista regime. On July 26, 1953, he began an insurrection, which failed. After a brief exile in Mexico, he returned to Cuba with an armed force and drove Batista out. He has been prime minister of Cuba since 1959.

Chou En-lai (1898?–1976): Born in Szechuan Province, of a Mandarin family, Chou studied in Paris and Germany. He helped to found the Chinese Communist party and the Chinese Red Army, and he took part in the Long March. Chou had been a member of the central committee of the party since 1926, and from 1949 he was premier of China.

Engels, Friedrich (1820–1895): Born in Barmen, Germany, the son of a textile manufacturer, he met Karl Marx in 1844. Three years later they wrote the *Communist Manifesto* and then founded the First International Workingmen's Association. Engels' last years were devoted to editing the second and third volumes of Marx's *Das Kapital,* as well as writing several books of his own.

Guevara, Dr. Ernesto (Che) (1928–1967): A native of Rosario, Argentina, he was educated as a physician. He was active in the opposition to the dictatorship of Perón in Argentina. Subsequently Guevara lived as a revolutionary in several South American nations and in Mexico, where he met and joined the exiled Cuban forces of Castro. After fighting successfully in the Cuban Revolution, Guevara was active in Cuban government affairs until 1965, when he left the island to return to guerrilla activities in South America. He was captured and executed by Bolivian government troops in 1967.

Hegel, Georg Wilhelm Friedrich (1770–1831): German idealist philosopher who influenced Marx and Engels, particularly with his theory that history was a process of thesis and antithesis making for struggle, which results in synthesis.

Ho Chi Minh (1890?–1969): His name means literally "he who shines"; his real name is uncertain. Born in Annam (now part of Vietnam), the son of a minor government official, at about nineteen Ho joined the crew of a French merchant ship, traveled the world for several years, and settled in Paris during World War I. He joined the Communist party and went to Moscow for political training. He was sent to China in 1925 and began his work of organizing a Communist underground of Vietnamese exiles. From 1946 he fought against the French in Vietnam until he was victorious, in 1964, and became president of the Democratic Republic of (North) Vietnam.

Kerenski, Alexander (1881–1970): Russian jurist, born in Simbirsk and educated at Tashkent and St. Petersburg University. He was briefly premier of the provisional government that existed in Russia after the February Revolution in 1917. After the Bolshevik victory in November 1917, Kerenski fled Russia, stayed in several countries, and after 1940 lived in the United States until his death.

Krushchev, Nikita Sergeevich (1894–1971): He was born in the village of Kalinovka in the Ukraine, worked on his father's farm, became a shepherd, miner, and locksmith. Khrushchev joined the Communist party in 1918, and not until 1920 did he receive his first formal education at a Communist party school in the factory where he worked. He rose persistently in Stalin's bureaucracy and prevailed in the power struggle in 1957 after Stalin's death.

He was premier of the USSR until 1964, when he was ousted for his too liberal views and policy failures. He was allowed to live peacefully in retirement until his death in 1971.

Kosygin, Aleksei (1904–   ): Born in St. Petersburg (now Leningrad), he received a technical education in textile manufacturing and became a shop superintendent in a Leningrad factory. His first important political post was that of manager of the industrial and transport department of the CPSU. Kosygin rose through a number of party and government offices. During World War II he was vice chairman of the Council of People's Commissars. He had been chairman of the USSR council of ministers since 1964.

Krumpskaya, Nadezhda Konstantinovna (1868–1939): Lenin's wife. They met at a pancake festival in 1894. When Lenin was sent to Siberia for his Communist activities she carried on his "League of Struggle" until she too was sent to Siberia, where they were married. Until Lenin's death in 1924 they worked closely together.

Lenin, Nicolai (Vladimir Illich Ulyanov) (1870–1924): The leader of the Russian Revolution, he was born in Simbirsk into a middle-class family. In 1891 he became a lawyer and in 1897 was exiled to Siberia for revolutionary activities. After his term ended he went to Europe and became the leader of the Bolshevik party. In 1917 he persuaded the German government to help him return to Russia and there he took over Marxist leadership. He ran the Soviet state until his death in 1924 and played a major role in the theoretical development of communism.

Mao Tse-tung (1893–1976): Mao was born into a peasant family in Hunan Province and educated as a teacher. He was a founding member of the Communist party of China in 1921 and active in education, youth organizations, and peasant unions. He led the Long March to escape the forces of Chiang Kai-shek and subsequently became the chairman of the Communist party.

Marx, Karl (1818–1883): The father of international communism, Marx was born in Germany. He studied law at the Bonn, Berlin, and Jena universities, and in 1843 was banished from Germany for his radical views. Banished from France, and then from Belgium, he fled to London in 1849. The year before, in Brussels, he published his *Communist Manifesto*. In the British Museum he worked on *Das Kapital*. The First International Workingmen's Association was organized by Marx and Engels in 1864. Until the end of his life he worked on *Capital,* only the first volume of which was published while he lived.

Plekhanov, Georgi (1857–1918): Second only to Lenin as Russian Marxist, he was instrumental in forming the first Russian Marxist party. He joined Lenin in editing the newspaper *Iskra.* The two split in 1903 with Plekhanov leading the Menshevik faction. He took no part in Russian revolution.

Stalin, Joseph (Iosif Vissarionovich Dzhugashvili) (1879–1953): Born the son of a shoemaker, Stalin was expelled from school for radicalism. By 1912 he was the editor of *Pravda.* His role in the revolution was minor but later as general secretary of the central committee he gained control of the party, defeating Trotsky in a struggle for power following Lenin's death. Thereafter Stalin ruled supreme in the USSR until his death in 1953.

Tito, Marshal (Josip Broz) (1892–   ): He was born in Zagorje, Croatia. He trained as a mechanic and served in the Austro-Hungarian Army in World War I and was imprisoned in Russian concentration camps. He took part in the Russian Revolution. Returned to Yugoslavia, he became active in trade union organization and in the Yugoslav Communist party. Tito fought in the Spanish Civil War, organized Yugoslav partisan resistance forces against the German occupation of Yugoslavia, and served as president of the National Liberation Committee. From 1945 to 1953 Tito was prime minister and since 1953 he has been president of the Republic of Yugoslavia.

Trotsky, Leon (Lev Davydovich Bronstein) (1877–1940): Born near Elisavetgrad, educated in Odessa, in 1898 Trotsky was banished to Siberia for revolutionary activities but escaped to London and joined Lenin. In 1903, however, he joined the Menshevik faction and did not rejoin Lenin politically until 1917. With Lenin in hiding after July 1917, Trotsky was in command of Bolshevik maneuvers that led to the October takeover of the Russian government. Later he created the Red Army while Stalin was gaining control of the party machinery. Their power struggle culminated in 1927 with Trotsky being expelled from the party and banished from the Soviet Union two years later. In 1940, while in exile in Mexico, he was murdered by Stalin's agents.

Bibliography of Sources

Aczel, Tamas, ed. *Ten Years After: The Hungarian Revolution in the Perspective of History.* New York: Holt, Rinehart and Winston, 1966.

Aguilar, Luis. *Marxism in Latin America.* New York: Alfred Knopf, 1968.

Brokhin, Yuri. *Hustling on Gorki Street.* New York: Dial Press, 1975.

Burg, David, and George Feifer. *Solzhenitsyn.* New York: Stein & Day, 1972.

Buss, Claude Albert. *The People's Republic of China and Richard Nixon.* San Francisco: W. H. Freeman, 1974.

Campbell, John C. *Tito's Separate Road.* New York: Harper & Row, 1967.

Carr, Edward. *The October Revolution; Before and After.* New York: Knopf, 1969.

Chai, Chu'u and Winberg Cahi. *The Changing Society of China.* New York: The New American Library, 1969.

Chen, I-fan. *Inside the Cultural Revolution.* New York: Macmillan, 1975.

Crow, John A. *Mexico Today.* New York: Harper and Brothers, 1957.

De Koster, Lester. *Vocabulary of Communism.* Grand Rapids, Michigan: William Eerdmans Publishing Co., 1964.

Dellin, L., ed. *Bulgaria.* New York: Praeger, 1957.

Deutsch, Andre. *Communist Economy Under Change.* London: The Institute of Economic Affairs, Rowan Press, 1963.

Deutscher, Isaac. *Communism.* New York: Oxford University Press, 1966.

————. *Marxism in Our Time.* Berkeley, California: Ramparts Press, 1971.

————. *The Prophet Armed, Trotsky 1879–1921.* New York: Oxford University Press, 1954.

————. *The Prophet Unarmed, Trotsky 1921–1929.* London, New York: Oxford University Press, 1959.

————. *The Prophet Outcast, Trotsky 1929–1940.* London, New York: Oxford University Press, 1963.

————. *Russia in Transition, and Other Essays.* New York: Coward-McCann, 1957.

————. *Stalin, a Political Biography.* London, New York: Oxford University Press, 1949.

————. *The Unfinished Revolution: Russia 1917–1967.* New York: Oxford University Press, 1967.

Dornberg, John. *The Other Germany.* Garden City, New York: Doubleday, 1968.

————. *The Soviet Union Today.* New York: Dial Press, 1976.

Draper, Theodore. *American Communism and Soviet Russia.* New York: The Viking Press, 1960.

Dumont, Rene. *Is Cuba Socialist?* New York: Viking Press, 1974.

Ebenstein, William. *Today's Isms.* Englewood Cliffs, New Jersey: Prentice-Hall, 1954.

Eliot, Alexander. *Greece.* New York: Life World Library, Time Inc., 1963.

Fan, Juang Huan. *From the Other Side of the River.* Garden City, New York: Anchor Press/Doubleday, 1975.

Fast, Howard. *The Naked God: The Writer and the Communist Party.* New York: Praeger, 1957.

Fessler, Loren. *China.* New York: Life World Library, Time Inc., 1963.

Floyd, David. *Rumania: Russia's Dissident Ally.* New York: Praeger, 1965.

Fremantle, Anne, ed. *Communism: Basic Writings.* New York: The New American Library, 1970.

Ginneken, Jaap van. *The Rise and Fall of Lin Piao.* New York: Avon Books, 1977.

Gretton, George, ed. *Communism and Colonialism.* New York: St. Martin's Press, 1964.

Han, Suyin, *Wind in the Tower—Mao Tse-tung and the Chinese Revolution 1949–1975.* Boston: Little Brown, 1976.

Harrison, J. F. C. *Quest for the New Moral World.* New York: Scribners, 1969.

Hendel, Samuel, ed. *The Soviet Crucible.* Princeton, New Jersey: D. Von Nostrand Co., 1959.

Herreshoff, David. *American Disciples of Marx.* Detroit: Wayne State University Press, 1967.

Hoffman, George, and Fred Werner Neal. *Yugoslavia and the New Communism.* New York: Twentieth Century Fund, 1962.

Houn, Franklin W. *A Short History of Chinese Communism.* Englewood Cliffs, New Jersey: Prentice-Hall, 1967.

Huberman, Leo, and Paul M. Sweenzy. *Socialism in Cuba.* New York: Monthly Review Press, 1969.

Karnow, Stanley. *Southeast Asia.* New York: Life World Library, Time, Inc., 1967.

Ketchum, Richard M., and Abraham Brunberg, eds. *What Is Communism?* New York: E. P. Dutton, 1963.

Kirkpatrick, Jeanne, J. ed. *The Strategy of Deception.* New York: Farrar, Straus & Giroux, 1963.

Koestler, Arthur. *Arrow in the Blue: An Autobiography.* New York: Macmillan, 1952–54.

———. *Darkness at Noon.* New York: Macmillan, 1941.

Kurzman, Dan. *Subversion of the Innocents.* New York: Random House, 1963.

Latham, Earl. *The Communist Controversy in Washington.* Cambridge, Massachusetts: Harvard University Press, 1966.

Lenin, Vladimir Il'ich. *State and Revolution.* London: Martin Lawrence, Ltd., 1933.

Leonhard, Wolfgang. *Three Faces of Marxism.* New York: Holt, Rinehart and Winston, 1974.

Lichtheim, George. *A Short History of Socialism.* New York: Praeger, 1970.

Lobkowicz, Nicholas, ed. *Marx and the Western World.* Notre Dame, Wisconsin: University of Notre Dame Press, 1967.

Lowenthal, Richard. *Model or Ally? The Communist Powers and the Developing Countries.* New York: Oxford Unixersity Press, 1977.

MacIntyre, Alasdair. *Marxism and Christianity.* New York: Schocken Books, 1968.

Manuel, Frank E., and P. Fritzie. *French Utopias.* New York: The Free Press, 1966.

Mao, Tse-tung. *Quotations from Chairman Mao Tse-tung.* Peking: Foreign Languages Press, 1966.

Marx, Karl. *Economy, Class and Social Revolution.* ed. Z. A. Jordan. New York: Scribner, 1975.

Matthews, Herbert Lionel. *Revolution in Cuba.* New York: Scribner, 1975.

McLellan, David. *Karl Marx.* New York: Viking, 1975.

Mihajlov, Mihajlo. *Underground Notes.* Kansas City, Kansas: Sheed, Andrews and McMeel, 1976.

Milton, David. *The Wind Will Not Subside.* New York: Pantheon, 1976.

————. *People's China.* New York: Random House, 1974.

Myrdal, Alva. *The Game of Disarmament.* New York: Pantheon, 1976.

Peterson, William, ed. *The Realities of World Communism.* Englewood Cliffs, New Jersey: Prentice-Hall, 1963.

Printz, Peggy, and Paul Steinle. *Commune: Life in Rural China.* New York: Dodd, Mead, 1977.

Reed, John. *Ten Days That Shook the World.* New York: Boni and Liveright, 1919.

Revel, Jean François. *The Totalitarian Temptation.* Garden City, New York: Doubleday, 1977.

Russell, Bertrand. *The Practice and Theory of Bolshevism.* New York: Simon and Schuster, 1964.

Scalapino, Robert A., ed. *The Communist Revolution in Asia.* Englewood Cliffs, New Jersey: Prentice-Hall, 1965.

Schatten, Fritz. *Communism in Africa.* New York: Praeger, 1966.

Schmitt, Karl M. *Communism in Mexico.* Austin, Texas: University of Texas Press, 1965.

Seybolt, Peter J. *Through Chinese Eyes.* New York: Praeger, 1974.

Smith, Hedrick. *The Russians.* New York: Ballantine Books, 1977 (paperback).

Solomon, Richard H. *A Revolution is Not a Dinner Party.* Garden City, New York: Doubleday/Anchor Press, 1975.

Solzhenitsyn, Alexander. *The Gulag Archipelago, 1918–1956.* New York: Harper & Row, 1974.

————. *Lenin in Zurich.* New York: Farrar, Straus & Giroux, 1976.

————. *Letter to the Soviet Leaders.* New York: Harper & Row, 1974.

————. *One Day in the Life of Ivan Denisovich.* New York: Praeger, 1963.

————. *Warning to the West.* New York: Farrar, Straus and Giroux, 1976.

Spielberg, Joseph, and Scott Whiteford, eds. *Forging Nations: A Comparative View of Rural Ferment and Revolt.* Michigan State University Press, 1976.

Starr, Richard F. *Poland 1944–1962.* Louisiana State University Press, 1962.

Stewart, Desmond. *The Arab World.* New York: Life World Library, Time, Inc., 1968.

Stillman, Edmund. *The Balkans.* New York: Life World Library, Time, Inc., 1964.

Swearingen, Rodger, ed. *Soviet and Chinese Communist Power in the World Today.* New York: Basic Books, 1966.

Swift, Lindsay. *Brook Farm.* New York: Corinth Books, 1961.

Trotsky, Leon. *The History of the Russian Revolution.* Ann Arbor, Michigan: University of Michigan Press, 1961.

————. *My Life.* Gloucester, Massachusetts: P. Smith, 1960.

————. *1905.* New York: Random House, 1971.

Watson, Hugh Seton. *From Lenin to Khrushchev.* New York: Praeger, 1960.

Wilson, Edmund. *To the Finland Station.* Garden City, New York: Doubleday, 1953.

Wilson, William E. *The Angel and the Serpent, the Story of New Harmony.* Bloomington, Indiana: Indiana University Press, 1964.

Index

Abraham Lincoln Brigade, 34
Acheampong, Ignatious K., 91–92
Africa. See Black African nations
Agriculture and communism, 17–18, 22–24, 55, 59, 72, 81, 93, 116–117, 121, 122, 127–128
Albania, 42, 56, 57, 61–62
Alessandri, Arturo, 121
Alexander II, Tsar, 10
Alexander III, Tsar, 10–11
Algeria, 83
Allende Gossens, Dr. Salvador, 122–123, 137
Alliance for Progress, 120, 123
American communism, 105–111
Andom, Aman Michael, 94
Andreotti, Guilio, 40
Angola, 92–93
Ankrah, Joseph, 91
Arab nations, 80–84; and Israel, 80, 82–83, 84; and Soviet Union, 82–84
Arbenz, Guzmán Joseph, 114
Aref, Abdul Salam, 83
Argentina, 111, 124
Aristotle, 13
Ashanti tribe, 91
Association of People's Owned Enterprises, 46
Aswan Dam, 82
Austria, 40
Avarado, Juan Velasco, 124

Balkans, 55–65
Bao Dai, 97
Barre, Mohammed Siyad, 93
Batista, Fulgencio, 115
Bay of Pigs invasion, 116
Becker, Jurek, 48
Belgian Congo. See Zaire
Belgium, 88
Benés, Eduard, 52
Benti, Tefari, 94
Beria, Levrenti, 20
Berlin blockade, 43
Berlin wall, 45
Berlinguer, Enrico, 40
Biermann, Wolf, 48
Black African nations, 84–95; and China, 85, 87; and Soviet Union, 85–87, 88–89, 89–90, 92–95
Bolivar, Simon, 123, 124
Bolivia, 124
Bolshevik, 12, 133
Bosia, Kofi A., 91
Brazil, 124
Brezhnev, Leonid I., 21–30, 53, 63, 128, 137
British Communist Party, 37, 39
British Labour Party, 37–38
Browder, Earl, 108–109
Broz-Tito, Jovanka, 60
Bulgaria, 56, 60–61

Cambodia, 98–99

Cambodian-Vietnamese border war, 98
Cárdenas, Lázaro, 113
Carrillo, Santiago, 38, 41
Carter, Jimmy, 52
Castro, Fidel, 115–119, 125, 137
Ceausescu, Nicolae, 63–64
Central America, 114–115
Chekhov, Anton Pavlovich, 53
Chiang Ch'ing, 75
Chiang Kai-shek, 67, 68, 87
Chile, 111–112, 120–123
China, 66–78, 102; and Black African nations, 85, 87; and Cuba, 118; and Southeast Asia, 98, 99, 101, 102, 104; and Soviet Union, 35–36, 70–71, 77; and United States, 19, 77
Chinese communism, 66–78
Chou En-lai, 75, 87, 137
Christian Democratic party, 39, 40, 121
Colonialism and communism, 79, 85–101, 113, 120, 129–130
Comecon, 63
Cominform, 34–35, 59, 134
Comintern, 31–34, 107, 108, 134
Commune, 1, 71, 72, 134
Communism: Chinese, 66–78; European, 31–65; future of, 21–30, 36, 41, 75–78, 103–104, 119, 123–132; history of, 1–21, 31–36, 66–75, 105–110; Latin American, 111–125, Russian, 10–36; Third World, 79–104; United States, 105–111
Communist Manifesto, Marx, 1, 6–7
Communist Party of India (CPI), 101–102
Costa Rica, 114
Cuba, 92, 94–95, 111–112, 115–119, 123; and Black African nations, 92, 94–95, 118–119; and China, 118; and Latin America, 117–118, 123; and Soviet Union, 115, 118, 119; and United States, 116, 118–119
Cuban missile crisis, 118
Cuban Revolution, 115
Cultural Revolution, 73–75
Cunhal, Alvaro, 40
Czechoslavakia, 52–54

Daily Worker, newspaper, 110
Das Kapital, Marx, 7, 11
Davis, Angela, 110
de Gaulle, Charles, 89
De Leon, Daniel, 106–107
Democratic socialism, 37–38
Denmark, 40
Dennis, Eugene, 110
Desai, Morarji, 102–103
d'Estaing, Valery Giscard, 39
Détente, 22
Dialectical materialism, 7–9, 134
Dictatorship of the proletariat, 2, 13–14
Die Revolution, magazine, 106
Djilas, Milovan, 60
Doctor Zhivago, Pasternak, 20
Dostoevski, Feodor Mikhlovich, 10
Dubček, Alexander, 53
Dudintsev, Vladimir, 20
Dulles, John Foster, 82

East Germany, 43–49
Eastern Europe, 41–55, 64–65
Egypt, 54, 81–83
El Salvador, 114
Engels, Friedrich, 1, 6, 7, 69, 137–138
England, 3, 7, 37–38, 39, 54, 101
Ethiopia, 93–95
Euro-communism, 2–3, 38–41
Euro-Communism and the State, Carrillo, 38
European communism, 31–65

Fabian Society, 37
Farouk I, King, 81
Ferdinand, Archduke Fanz, 59
Ferrer, José Figueres, 114
Five-year plan, 17–18, 24, 134
Ford, Gerald, 52
Ford, James, 110
Foster, William, 109, 110
France, 39, 54, 97
Franco, Francisco, 33
Freedom fighters, 54
Frei, Eduardo, 122
French Communist Party, 39
Future of communism, 21–30, 36, 41, 75–78, 103–104, 119, 123–132

Galanskov, Yuri, 25
Gandhi, Indira, 102, 103
Gandhi, Mohandas Karamshand, 101
Garvey, Marcus, 91
Gates, John, 110
German Democratic Republic (DDR), 43–49
Germany, 19, 31, 33, 34. See also East Germany, West Germany
Ghana, 90–92
Giereck, Edward, 51–52
Ginzburg, Alexsandr, 25
Gomulka, Wladislaw, 51
Great Leap Forward, 71–73, 135
Greece, 56–57
Guatemala, 114
Guevera, Dr. Ernesto (Che), 118, 138
Guinea, 89–90

Haile Selassie, Emperor, 94
Hall, Gus, 110
Hegel, Georg Wilhelm Friedrich, 6, 7, 138
Helsinki accords, 26, 53
History of communism, 1–21, 31–36, 66–75, 105–110
Hitler, Adolf, 32, 43, 50, 51, 63
Ho Chi Minh, 97, 138
Honduras, 114
Honecker, Erich, 49
Hoxha, Enver, 61–62
Hsüan-t'ung, Emperor, 67
Hua Kuo-feng, 75, 77
Hungarian revolt, 54
Hungary, 31, 54–55
Husak, Gustav, 53

Imperialism, 35, 86, 135
India, 101–103
Indonesia, 100–101
Industrial Revolution, 1–2, 6
Industrial Workers of the World (IWW), 107, 135
Industry and communism, 1–2, 6, 8, 17, 23, 24–25, 28–29, 45–46, 55, 59, 63–64, 72, 117, 121, 126–128
International Macedonian Revolutionary Organization (MRO), 61
International Workingmen's Association, 9, 31

Internationals, 9, 31–32, 38, 135
Iraq, 83
Israel and Arab nations, 80, 82–83, 84
Italy, 33, 38–40

Jacobin, 125, 135
Japan, 33, 69, 99
Juárez, Benito, 113

Kádár, Janos, 55
Karamanlis, Konstantinos, 57
Kennedy, John F., 120, 127
Kerenski, Alexander, 12, 138
Khieu, Samphan, 99
Khrushchev, Nikita Sergeevich, 20–21,
Kim Il-Sung, 100
Kissinger, Henry, 83
Korea, 19, 99–100
Korean War, 19, 69, 100
Krumpskaya, Nadezhda Konstantinovna, 15, 139
25, 35, 57, 59, 61, 62, 70–71, 86, 118, 138–139
Kulak, 17–18, 135
Kuomintang, 67, 68, 69

Lafargue, Paul, 111
Laos, 98
Latin America, 111–125; and Cuba, 117–118, 123; and United States, 114–115, 116, 121
Latin American communism, 111–125
Lenin, Nicolai (Vladimer Ulyanov), 3, 10–14, 16, 17, 27, 32, 38, 46, 53, 70, 86, 128, 139
Levellers, 5
Libya, 83
Li Jong-ok, 100
Locke, John, 4–5
Lon Nol, 99
Long March, 68
Lumumba, Patrice, 88
Lvov, Prince George, 12
Lysenko, Trofim, 23

Malenkov, Georgi, 20
Manchus, 66–67
Mao Tse-tung, 35–36, 56, 66, 68–75, 76, 78, 139

Maoism, 70–71, 129, 135
Marchais, George, 39
Mariam, Mengistu Haile, 94
Marx, Karl, 1–3, 6–9, 13, 16, 17, 24, 27, 28, 31, 37, 38, 46, 69, 70, 85–86, 105, 106, 126–127, 128, 139
Marxism, 1–3, 6–9, 13–14, 16, 23, 35, 117, 131–132
Masaryk, Jan, 52
McCarthy investigations, 109
Mella, Julio Antonio, 112
Menshevik, 12, 135
Mexican communist parties, 112, 113–114
Mexican Revolution, 112
Mexico, 112–114
Middle East, 80–84
Mihajlov, Mihajlo, 60
Mihajlović, Draža, 58
Mikoyan, Anastas, 90
Ming dynasty, 66
Mittag, Günter, 46
Mitterrand, François, 39
Mobutu, Joseph, 88
Molotov, Vyacheslav Michailovich, 20, 108
More, Sir Thomas, 4
Mutual defense pact (German-Soviet), 34, 108

Nagy, Imre, 54
Nasser, Gamal Abdel, 81–82
Nationalism and communism, 3, 31, 58, 85, 130
Nehru, Jawaharlal, 102
Netherlands, 100
Neto, Agostinho, 92–93
Ngo Dinh Diem, 94
Nicaragua, 114
Nicholas II, Tsar, 11–13
Nixon, Richard M., 77
Nkrumah, Kwame, 90–91
Not By Bread Alone, Dudintsev, 20

October War, 82
O'Higgins, Bernardo, 120
Ongania, Juan Carlos, 124
Overpopulation (Chinese), 77–78
Owen, Robert, 105–106

Padillo, Heberto, 119
Palestine Liberation Organization (PLO), 84
Pan-African movement, 85
Panama, 114–115
Parasite law (Soviet), 27
Pasternak, Boris, 20
People's Republic of China. See China
Perón, Juan, 124
Peru, 124
Plato, 4
Plekhanov, Georgi, 11, 139–140
Poland, 50–52
Politiburo, 15–16, 135
"Popular Democracies," 42–43
Popular Front, 32
Portugal, 40–41, 92–93, 111
Pravda, newspaper, 15, 23–24, 135
Proletarian Armed Guards, 39
Proletariat, 8, 86, 136

Quotations From Chairman Mao Tse-tung, 70

Rákosi, Mátyás, 42, 54
Rapp, George, 105–106
Recabarren, Luis Emilio, 112
Red Brigades, 39
Red Guard, 73–74
Religion and communism, 51, 80, 85, 93, 128–129
Republic, Plato, 4
Republic of China. See China
Revel, Jean-François, 41
Revisionism, 109, 136
Rhodesia, 95
Roberto, Holden, 88
Rodrigues, Jorge Alessandri, 121–122
Romania, 56, 62–64
Rosenberg case, 109
Rousseau, Jean Jacques, 5
Roy, Manabendra Narth, 112
Russia, 10–30. See also Soviet Union
Russian communism, 10–36
Russian Revolution, 12–13

Sadat, Anwar el, 81, 82, 83
Sakharov, Andrei, 29
Samizdat, 25

Samoza, Anastasio, 114
San Martin, José de, 124
Saudi Arabia, 83, 93–94
Shang dynasty, 66
Shaw, George Bernard, 37
Shermarke, Abdulrashid Ali, 93
Sihanouk, Prince Norodom, 99
Social Contract, Rousseau, 5
Solod, Daniel, 89–90
Solzhenitsyn, Alexander, 25
Somalia, 93–95
Souphanouvong, Prince, 98
South Yemen, 83
Southeast Asia, 95–104; and China, 98, 99, 101, 102, 104; and Soviet Union, 97–98, 99, 101, 102, 104
Souvanna Phouma, Prince, 98
Soviet, 11, 136
Soviet Union, 13–30, 31–32, 33–34; and Arab nations, 82–84; and Black African nations, 85–87, 88–89, 89–90, 92–95; and China, 35–36, 70–71, 77; and Cuba, 115, 118, 119; and Southeast Asia, 97–98, 99, 101, 102, 104; and United States, 19, 22, 118, 131. *See also* Russia
Spain, 33–34, 38, 108, 111, 120
Spanish Civil War, 33–34, 108
Spartacus, 4
Stalin, Joseph (Iosiph Vissarionovich Dzhugashvili), 3, 15–19, 20, 22, 24, 26, 32–33, 35, 43, 44, 45, 50, 54, 58–59, 61, 65, 70, 86, 107, 108, 109–110, 128, 140
Stalin, Trotsky, 15
Stalinism, 15–19, 20–21, 29, 44–45
Stambuliski, Alexander, 61
Strategic Arms Limitation Talks (SALT), 22
Students for a Democratic Society (SDS), 111
Suez crisis, 54
Suharto, President, 101
Sukarno, Achmed, 100–101
Sun Yat-sen, 67
Supreme Soviet, 16, 136
Surplus value, 24, 25, 136
Syria, 83

Taiwan, 77

Teng Hsiao-ping, 75
Third world communism, 79–104
Three Sisters, Chekhov, 53
Tibet, 130
Tito, Marshal (Josip Broz), 58–60, 61, 62, 140
Titoism, 58–60
Togliatti, Palmiro, 40
Tolstoi, Count Leo, 10
Torres, Juan José, 124
Totalitarian Temptation, Revel, 41
Touré, Sékou, 89–90, 91
Trotsky, Leon (Lev Bronstein), 12, 14–16, 113, 140
Trotskyism, 15–16, 136
Tupamaros, 125
Turkey, 56

Ugarte, Augusto Pinochet, 123
Ulbricht, Walter, 43, 44, 49
Ulyanov, Alexander, 10–11
Union of Soviet Socialist Republics (USSR). See Soviet Union
United States, 33–34, 40, 57, 95, 99–100, 103–111, 114–115; and China, 19, 77; and Cuba, 116, 118–119; and Latin America, 114–115, 116, 121; and Soviet Union, 19, 22, 118, 131.
University of the Eastern Toilers, Tashkent, USSR, 86
Uraguay, 125
Ustinov, Marshal Dmitri, 29

Vietnam, 97–98
Vietnam War, 97
Vietnamese-Cambodian border war, 98

Webb, Beatrice, 37
Webb, Sydney, 37
Wells, H. G., 37
West Germany, 40
Western Europe, 37–41
Weydemeyer, Joseph, 106
What Is to Be Done?, Lenin, 12
Woodhull, Victoria, 106
World War I, 12, 54, 58–59, 61
World War II, 19, 24, 42–43, 54, 57–58, 61

Yakobsen, Anatoly, 21
Yezhov, 18
Yezhovchina, 18–19, 136
Yüan Shih-k'ai, 67

Yugoslavia, 42, 56, 57–60

Zaire, 88–89
Zhivkov, Todor, 61

About the Author

James D. Forman is a well-known author of books for young people, among them *Shield of Achilles, Ring the Judas Bell,* and *My Enemy, My Brother.* The last two titles were honored in the *Book World* Spring Book Festival in the year of their publication.

Mr. Forman is a graduate of Princeton University and Columbia University Law School. He has traveled widely in Europe, especially in Greece, a country that has served as background for a number of his books. Mr. Forman lives on Long Island. His other Watts titles include *Inflation, Nazism,* and three other Studies in Contemporary Politics books: *Anarchism, Fascism,* and *Socialism.* Most recently he has written *Freedom's Blood,* a fictional reconstruction of the shocking murders of three civil rights workers in Mississippi during the summer of 1964.